Assessment

Getting it right ✓

IN A WEEK

Martin Fautley & Alison Daubney
Series editor: **Susan Wallace**

Copyright © (2017) Martin Fautley and Alison Daubney

British Library Cataloguing in Publication Data

A CIP record for this book is available from the British Library

ISBN: 978-1-911106-30-2

This book is also available in the following e-book format:
MOBI: 978-1-911106-31-9

The rights of Martin Fautley and Alison Daubney to be identified as the Authors of this work have been asserted by them in accordance with the Copyright, Design and Patents Act 1988.

Illustrations © (2017) Michael Wallace
Cover and text design by Out of House Limited

Project management by Out of House Publishing Solutions

Typeset by Out of House Publishing Solutions

Printed and bound in Great Britain by TJ International, Padstow

Critical Publishing
3 Connaught Road
St Albans
AL3 5RX

www.criticalpublishing.com

For orders and details of our bulk discounts please go to our website www.criticalpublishing.com or contact our distributor NBN International by telephoning 01752 202301 or emailing orders@nbninternational.com.

MIX
Paper from
responsible sources
FSC® C013056

CONTENTS

Martin Fautley

I am Director of Research in the School of Education and Social Work at Birmingham City University. I have a wealth of experience in music education, both in terms of pedagogy and music education research. After enjoying many years as a classroom music teacher, I then undertook full-time doctoral research working across the education and music faculties at the University of Cambridge, investigating teaching, learning and assessment of classroom music-making, with a focus on composing as a classroom activity. I research understandings of musical learning and progression, composing and creativity, and am the author of eight books, and over 50 journal articles, book chapters and academic research papers on a range of aspects of teaching and learning.

Alison Daubney

I am a senior teaching fellow in education at the University of Sussex. I am an experienced teacher, researcher, mentor, teacher educator and workshop leader across formal and non-formal education. I have worked extensively on international assessment and curriculum development with Cambridge International Examinations. In 2008 I was awarded a PhD from the University of Surrey, Roehampton. My research is widely published and relates to assessment, technology, musical engagement of children in challenging circumstances and anxiety in performance domains.

Susan Wallace

I am Emeritus Professor of Education at Nottingham Trent University where part of my role has been to support trainee teachers on initial and in-service teacher training courses. My own experience of classroom teaching has been mainly with 14- to 19-year-olds; and I have also worked in a local authority advisory role for this age group. My particular interest is in the motivation and behaviour management of reluctant and disengaged learners, and I've written a number of books and research papers on this topic. My work allows me the privilege of meeting, observing and listening to teachers from all sectors of education. It is to them that I owe many of the ideas contained in this series of books.

Assessment. A term often unjustly truncated to mean 'tracking' or 'accountability'; ironic, really, considering that the power of assessment is at the centre of our in-the-moment interactions with the world inside and outside the classroom. It is time to reconsider the breadth of the term *assessment* and how it is a fundamentally important tool across learning and teaching. In this book we aim to do just that!

Assessment is a vital part of education today. Indeed, it is so closely linked with education that for many people, assessment has come to dominate their lives. One of the biggest misconceptions is that assessment is *only* about testing. We want to show how although testing – a type of summative assessment – is important, it is formative assessment which makes a very real difference to the learning of those you teach. Throughout this book we want to show you that assessment is not something that should be your master, but your servant, and that it is not something you should worry about, but something you should embrace so as to help your learners.

Assessment as a term has a very broad application, and encompasses a whole raft of ideas and concepts. Historically, it was often assumed that assessment was somehow separated from teaching and learning (Graue, 1993); but we want to show that assessment can and should be a part of your normal everyday teaching. It can sometimes feel as though assessment in the form of testing is all that seems to matter nowadays. We are sure that many teachers did not enter the profession simply to give tests, but to share the joy of learning with young people. This book will hopefully help you to think about how you can do this.

One of the key things we have been at pains to observe in this book is that you are the expert in your own particular context. You know your learners, your setting, your context, your community. Assessment sometimes is presented as context-free, but we want to point out that there are aspects which you can take control of, and that you always need to bear in mind that you will know best how to personalise things to suit your purpose for your learners and yourself. This is not to say that national standards do not matter, far from it, but that in preparing your learners to be able to meet the exacting national standards required of them today, you need to start from where they are. It is your own assessments of the situation that will enable you to do this successfully.

In this book we will be presenting some strategies and responding to current educational challenges. Throughout, we hope to show you what assessment could look like, and how a variety of assessment approaches can be employed in a variety of educational settings. We will offer you a straightforward toolkit of ideas, presented through day-to-day ideas and activities. Due to time limitations in the lives of busy teachers everywhere, this book is designed to be used over one week, and is short and straight to the point. So you can take a deep breath and just enjoy exploring what assessment can mean for you and your learners.

Who is this book for?

Whatever setting you work in or age group you teach, there is much in this book for you. Whether you are new to teaching or a more experienced teacher or lecturer, you will find strategies and ideas that will enhance your thinking and teaching. Assessment permeates teaching, whether in pre-school, primary, secondary, further or higher education. The strategies and ideas discussed can be flexibly used across subject areas and contexts. The term *learners* is used throughout rather than pupil or student because it is universally applicable.

How this book is set out

The book is divided into seven chapters, one chapter for each day of the week. Each chapter has a range of strategies for you to try. Some strategies are separated into sub-sections so that you can experiment with different approaches and see which one works best for you. Following each strategy is a scenario showing how it might look in practice, and there are also some reflective questions to help you think about how you might incorporate these into your own teaching. The *A Spot of Theory* section helps to underpin and support these strategies and there are many of these throughout the book. There is also a *Further reading* section at the end of the book should you wish to learn more about the theoretical background, or for references in your studies.

What's in it?

The first chapter, **Day 1**, asks one of the most important assessment questions: 'What's this *formative* stuff?' This is followed by exploring what it means for you, your learners, your school and what it could look like in your classroom. **Day 2** is concerned with thinking about learning, and asks you to reflect on how some assessments are derived from the curriculum. **Day 3** discusses the place and purpose of tests and quizzes, and how you can use these within the classroom. **Day 4** asks the really important question: 'Who is the assessment for?' It is important because knowing the answer can determine in some ways the types of assessment open to you. How assessment can be used to improve learning is discussed in **Day 5**, and you will also think about using assessment data for planning purposes. **Day 6**, 'You need some grades, now!' deals with issues associated with testing, but also looks at comparative judgement as a way of making your assessment work more manageable. The final day, **Day 7**, sets out some useful techniques for different forms of assessment use, put together for you as a practitioner.

How might you use it?

This book is designed to be read easily, simple to use, and easy to reference and relate directly to educational practice. Some scenarios may make you question your own practice, amuse you, or be very familiar. Hopefully throughout the book you will consider new insights and be open to new possibilities! Ultimately, this book aims to build your confidence so that you will develop that in your learners.

Because we know time is limited, you will find towards the end of each chapter just one suggested strategy, out of the ones outlined, presented under the heading, *If you only try one thing from this chapter, try this*. We hope over time you will try as many strategies as possible and really explore what assessment means for you and your learners in the classroom. To help identify your next steps, each chapter ends with a checklist, which enables you to note down what you have tried, what worked best for you and with whom.

There is a lot of jargon in education, as well as words having what might be termed as 'slippery' meanings. *Formative assessment* is one of those! There has been a great deal of research into formative assessment, and a lot of school and other policies published too, but this does not mean its meaning is entirely clear! One of the many issues with formative assessment is what to actually call it. The term *assessment for learning*, often abbreviated to AfL, is one of its many other names. While there can be a dispute as to whether AfL and formative assessment are identical, for the purposes of this book, we will treat them as being the same thing.

What, no numbers?

For too many people in education, assessment has come to mean only testing and test scores. In today's strategies, we want to think about how you can use formative assessment to help you in your teaching, and, importantly, to help your learners move forward with their learning. Formative assessment should be absolutely about you and the learners in your classroom, and the clear communication between you and them. This is the key take-away for today. Formative assessment, done properly, does not have to involve numbers or grades (although it can; but that's up to you) or marking learners' work three times using different coloured pens each time. No, it should be about *you*, what you say to the learners, and what they say to you. Good formative assessment can be as simple as having a conversation with your learners.

Today's strategies

1. Listening in – listen to learners talking to each other about work

2. Discussion not monologue – talking with, not at, the learners

3. Traffic lights – learners show you what they can/can't do

4. If I had five more minutes – how would learners' work improve if they had just a little more time? (try it!)

5. Why questions – why are we learning this?

Strategy: Listening in – listen to learners talking to each other about work

Introduction

Although you should be the centre of attention in a classroom, there are likely to be times when you want your learners to be working on something themselves without your direct input. How you manage this is completely up to you, and, possibly, your school policies. But assuming your learners do talk to each other in class during a task, what are they saying? We know that talking things through helps learning, and develops understanding, so this formative assessment strategy will help with this.

1. Listening in

Learning is complex, complicated, multifaceted, and definitely not simple and straightforward! There are times when you will want your learners to be getting on with something without you talking all the time. What happens when you do this? Do you lurk noticeably by learners you are concerned about? Do you walk around the room giving help to learners who need it? For this strategy you need to be in a position to listen to the learners as they talk about what they are doing. For some teachers, the hardest part of this is not butting in straight away but allowing a bit of time to elapse before intervening. The purpose of this strategy is to develop your understanding and evaluation of the impact of what it is that you have asked the learners to do through observing them working and discussing. In an ideal world, of course, every teacher would only have to explain something once, and all the learners would 'get it' straight away. Sadly, we know this is not often the case. So, what happens once you have set the learners off to do whatever it is you have asked them? Are they having detailed learning conversations? Are they floundering a bit? Have they all understood? What about that difficult group you've sat at the front? Do they 'get it'?

This is not an easy 'sit back and listen' strategy, as the next stage requires you to actually do something with the information you have gathered.

✸ What are you going to do next, in terms of teaching and learning? Have they mastered the groundwork sufficiently to proceed? Are there common misconceptions you need to address? If you are due to teach this lesson again to another class, are there things that you might need to consider doing differently?

The assessment for learning decisions you take here are key to progress both today and in the future, but what have *you* learned by listening in?

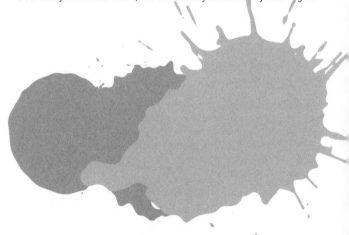

Mrs Khan has set her class some mathematics work in pairs. As they do the exercises from the books, she walks round the room, spending, it seems, a long time tidying the cupboard at the side of the classroom, but in actual fact she is listening in to some learners nearby.

" *'I just don't see what to do'*, says Darren.

" *'Look at the numbers'*, says Harjinder, sitting next to him. *'You just take this one and times it by that one.'*

" *'Yes but why?'* asks Darren.

" *'I don't know, but that's what you do'*, replies Harjinder.

" *'OK, but I still don't see why!'* Darren retorts.

" Mrs Khan moves her attention to another group.

" *'Did you get this answer?'* asks Janie.

" *'No'*, says Danielle. *'Are you sure that's right?'*

" *'No, I'm not!'* answers Janie. *'Let's do it between us and see what we get.'*

* What conclusions would you draw if you were Mrs Khan?
* Why might the fact that Darren doesn't know why he has to multiply the numbers be an issue?
* How does Mrs Khan know whether Harjinder really understands what to do? What about Janie and Danielle?
* Now, think about this in the context of your own classroom. What could you do to try this approach with your own teaching and learning?
* What's stopping you?

A Spot of Theory

Vygotsky defines the notion of the zone of proximal development *(ZPD) as:*

the distance between the actual developmental level as determined by independent problem solving and the level of potential development as determined through problem solving under adult guidance, or in collaboration with more capable peers.

(Vygotsky, 1978, p 86)

In this strategy, the learners are learning from both the teacher, and their 'more capable peers', so lots of ZPD is taking place!

Strategy: Discussion not monologue – talking with, not at, the learners

Introduction

One of the key ways in which you can develop formative assessment with your learners is to talk with them. The previous strategy involved listening in; this one asks you to think about having conversations with your learners. This is neither as simple nor as obvious as it sounds.

2. Discussion not monologue

✸ When do you talk to someone else? For example, your partner, your friends, your mum? Do you talk *to* them, or *with* them? Do they talk to you, or with you? What does listening to other people involve?

These aren't meant to be deep and meaningful questions – although they could be! Do conversations you have with your adult social group differ from those you have with young learners? We hope so! But what about you the teacher as turn-taker in a conversation? One aspect of formative assessment is that teacher and learner discuss together what learning is going on, and work out between them what the next steps are in the learning that the individual learner can do. This does not mean that all teaching has to stop while you have individual conversations with every child that you teach, but that this is a 'stolen time' opportunity, when the class are working on a task, giving you a chance for a one-to-one discussion.

Conversations between teacher and learner are not as simple as you might think! There are power relationships at play, and interpersonal dynamics too. As the Assessment Reform Group noted some years ago, *'Learners need information and guidance in order to plan the next steps in their learning. Teachers should: pinpoint the learner's strengths and advise on how to develop them...'* (Assessment Reform Group, 2002, p 4). This can be done by talking *with* learners. Listening to what they have to say is an important part of this formative assessment strategy. As we know:

> *One way of asking a question might produce no answer from the student, while a slightly different approach may elicit evidence of achievement. We can never be absolutely sure that we have exhausted all the possibilities, so that we can never be sure that the student does not know something, but some assessments will be better than others in this respect.*

(Wiliam and Black, 1996, p 541)

So, in order to try to find out what the learners know and might not know, we talk *with* them, not to them.

Mr Henrik teaches physics in a secondary school. Every few lessons he likes to set the learners on a practical task, and then walk round the classroom talking to them about what they are doing. But he is not just asking them about the work they are doing in today's lesson; he also wants to talk to them about how the work they are doing now fits with the scheme of work for the term.

Mr Henrik: *Hey, Sophie, you've got all the equipment set up I see.*

Sophie: *Yes, but I had a bit of trouble doing it!*

Mr Henrik: *Oh, why's that then?*

Sophie: *I couldn't get the switch to work.*

Mr Henrik: *Do you remember when we did light bulbs last term?*

Sophie: *Err, I think so.*

Mr Henrik: *Did you manage to get your lights to switch on and off?*

Sophie: *Yes, I remember now.*

Mr Henrik: *What did we say about the switch then?*

Sophie: *Oh I remember, the wires had not got to touch each other.*

Mr Henrik: *Have a look at your circuit board now.*

Sophie: *Oh, duh...*

This is a simple example of an AfL dialogue. This looks all very normal, but note two things.

- Firstly, Mr Henrik does not just tell Sophie that the wires are touching – although he could (and some teachers would argue he should, as this will save time) – but he talks her through the cumulative learning that has taken place over the course of a series of lessons on this topic.

- Secondly, what Mr Henrik is doing here is to establish what Sophie knows, and what connections she needs to make in order to be able to undertake the task in hand, building on her prior learning. He does this by helping her make a connection with prior learning, and therefore build her own conceptual framework of understanding.

It will depend on you, your learners, and your school policy, but AfL discussions of this nature (and this is a very simple one) can have a strong impact on learning.

A Spot of Theory

One of the early writers on formative assessment noted that 'The essential conditions for improvement are that the student comes to hold a concept of quality roughly similar to that held by the teacher...' (Sadler, 1989, p 121). But quality can be itself a problematic construct. By talking with Sophie, Mr Henrik is able to help her understand what she has to do, and to see how a 'quality' solution can be arrived at.

Strategy: Traffic lights – learners show you what they can/can't do

Introduction

The American politician Donald Rumsfeld famously said, *'There are things that we know we don't know. But there are also unknown unknowns. There are things we don't know we don't know'*. For AfL to be successful, we need to help the learners towards knowing what they don't know. It is, of course, much harder to get them to think about what they don't know that they don't know, so let's start with thinking about the former!

3. Traffic lights

Traffic lights, also known in some contexts as the RAG rating (RAG = Red, Amber, Green), is a way of equipping your learners with a simple visual strategy for demonstrating to you in either an overt or an unobtrusive way whether or not they think they understand a topic. What it entails is the learners being equipped with some form of visual indicator using the three traffic light colours, for example small laminated cards or stickers. Some schools have adopted this system across the school, and have given out learning diaries which have red, amber and green pages included.

When a learner thinks they understand something, they display the green 'light'; when they are not quite sure, the amber; and when they know they don't understand, the red. This can be done in many ways. In some cases, the teacher asks the learners to simply hold up the appropriate colour to indicate where they think their understandings lie. This is, of course, a very public display, and some learners may be reluctant to demonstrate uncertainty at this level in front of their peers. In some schools – particularly primary – the learners are asked to close their eyes as they hold up the cards, so they can't see how others have responded. In order to address this, another way of using the traffic lights system is for the learners to simply have the red or amber card turned face-up during times when the teacher is moving around the classroom. This enables the teacher to intervene in more subtle ways in order to help the individual learners who require it.

Used regularly, the traffic lights can become an integral way of you being able to offer assistance in a timely fashion where it is required, and to undertake a quick visual scan of how understandings are going in the moment of the lesson. The two methods of using the cards are not mutually exclusive; both can be employed in the same classroom, as can other variations.

Miss Wood teaches in a primary school. All of her learners have a notebook which she likes them to keep on their desk at all times to make notes and jottings as they think of them. She has printed and laminated a set of traffic light cards (about the size of a credit card) for each of the learners in her class. Today she is teaching a lesson on multiplication, and has explained how she want the learners to do the sums she has set. Having explained an example on the board, she then asks each learner to hold up the card which best summarises what they think about their own understanding. Miss Wood notices that she has a large number of amber and red cards being held up, many more than green cards. She decides that she will work through another example on the board for all of the class. She does, and then repeats the request for a display of traffic lights. This time there is a much greater number of green cards, and so Miss Wood decides that she will concentrate her attention on the learners who displayed amber and red cards.

Miss Wood organises the learners who displayed red and amber cards to work at a table at the side of the classroom, while those who displayed green cards are set to work in the rest of the room. This enables Miss Wood to get on with further explanations and examples for this specific group of learners, while she can still keep an eye on those who believe they understand.

Doing this, Miss Wood feels, enables her to target her scaffolded support at the learners who are most in need at that moment, and allows her to maximise her precious time in an organised and efficient fashion.

A Spot of Theory

Bruner's notion of scaffolding (Wood et al, 1976) is important here as it describes how a teacher can support learning by offering support when it is needed. Importantly, Bruner also describes how the scaffolding of teacher interventions can be withdrawn as learning becomes more secure.

Strategy: If I had five more minutes – how would learners' work improve if they had just a little more time? (try it!)

Introduction

You will be very well used to working according to strict times and timeframes. In many schools, the passing of time is marked by bells or buzzers, and teachers and learners both know that this means the end of something, and the beginning of something else. But what would happen if you were to subvert this; obviously you probably can't change the times of the bells without causing major disruption, but what happens if you allow just a few more minutes for a task?

4. If I had five more minutes

This strategy can be used in all settings, but requires different tactics for its management depending on how the day is organised. In a primary school, with a single teacher in charge of the class for much of the day, it will be easier than in a secondary school, academy or college, where there are different demands and requirements. But there are a number of ways of achieving this.

One way of using this strategy addresses a common problem in schools, where we tell learners how they could do better at a piece of work that they've just done, but are unlikely to do again! Using our strategy, however, the learners finish their work as normal, have it marked and graded, and then handed back to them with the opportunity in class to spend five minutes (or whatever time is appropriate) addressing the issues

that the teacher has pointed out. The work is then handed in again, with improvements noted. This doesn't mean that you have to mark the entire piece again, simply the new material.

Another way of employing this strategy is to allow your learners to finish their work as usual, and then have some other form of activity, break-time, or learning encounter; then, next time the lesson comes round, begin by spending an extra five minutes giving attention to the piece of work again. This enables the learners to revisit and check through their work before finally completing it.

A third way of using this strategy in performance-based subjects, including (but not limited to) music and drama, allows the learners to finish and show their work, after which they are told they have an extra five minutes to just revisit the performance (or other work) with a view to tidying up any loose ends. Then a revised performance can take place, with – hopefully – the benefits of the extra time showing. In performance-based subjects it is useful to have an audio or video recording to refer back to in order to decide what might be useful. Another very important way to use it is to let learners think through and explain what/how/why they would do something differently, even if there is insufficient time to actually do it. This gets them thinking about the *process* of learning, rather than thinking they have to come up with another end product. This discussion (which links back to Strategy 1) helps you understand their thought process and creative ideas.

What does *five more minutes* mean in the context of your subject? We are aware that this book will be read by many different teachers of a variety of subjects and age ranges, so, what does it mean for you?

- What would five more minutes involve...
  1. in written work?
  2. across two lessons?
  3. in practical lessons?
  4. when you only see the learners for one lesson a week?
  5. when you see the learners every day?
  6. when you see the learners all day, every day?
  7. when you finish early?
  8. when you want them to have more time?
  9. when you want the *quality* of the work to improve?
  10. when you want the *quantity* of the work to increase?

- Think about these questions, and try to come up with ways in which you can implement this strategy with your class.

Why is it a formative assessment strategy? The answer to this question is that by giving formative feedback, either spoken or written, you are helping the learners take that important next step in what they will be doing. This is an *immediate* next step, and is built on what they are doing in the here and now. This involves the learners in *metacognition*, in other words, in thinking about their own thinking.

" What would I improve if I had five more minutes?"

A Spot of Theory

Harlen and James (1997, p 206) note that: 'When something is learned with understanding (deep learning, 'real' learning) it is actively understood and internalised by the learner. It makes sense in terms of a learner's experience of the world...'. *Learning with understanding – deep learning – is a useful notion for acquisition and employment in the classroom.*

Strategy: Why questions – why are we learning this?

Introduction

Have you ever had the experience of a learner asking you, *'Why are we doing this?'* If you have, you will know that learners do not always have the same overview of a teaching and learning programme, programme of study, or scheme of work in their heads as you do in yours! Answering such questions with, *'Because I said so'*, or, *'Because it's on the syllabus'* may not be the most satisfactory answer for learners. This strategy turns the question around, and asks the learners what they think.

5. Why questions

When we begin a new topic, or move to a different area of teaching and learning, as educators we often begin this process by telling the learners both *what* they will be learning and doing, and *why* they will be learning and doing it. In this strategy we pick this up a little way into the teaching and learning programme, and ask the learners themselves to explain why they are doing a particular activity. *'Because we have to'* is not acceptable as a suitable answer!

This strategy requires the learners to be able to make connections with their prior learning, and, depending on how aware they are of what is coming next, will also act as a stepping-stone to future work. The learners need to be able to take a step back from the immediacy of the lesson, and think about it in the context of a series of lessons, looking both forward and behind. This is not as common as you might think in terms of how we interact with our learners. It is another form of metacognition, asking learners to think about their own thinking.

Encouraging learners to ask 'why' questions

The class in a secondary-school science lesson are learning about looking at things using a microscope. The teacher has prepared a series of slides for the learners to look at through the microscope and describe what they see. There has been much of what the teacher describes as 'faffing about' as the learners get to grips with using the microscopes and actually being able to see something down them! After a while, the teacher stops the class, and asks them, *'Why do you think we are doing this?'* Here are some of the answers she gets.

" *So we know how to use a microscope.*

" *Because I saw them using one on CSI last week.*

" *Because you said we are studying cells next.*

" *Because we can't see things this tiny without one.*

" *Because proper scientists use microscopes.*

" *Because it's on the exam.*

" *So we know it's not a telescope.*

Here are some reflective questions for you to think about relating to the answers the teacher received:

✷ Which of these answers do you think the teacher should develop in her response?

✷ How important in developing learners is knowledge of what is to come?

✷ Which of these would you say is the 'best' answer? (This is subjective, and there is no right answer!)

✷ And which the 'worst'? (Ditto!)

✷ Are there any answers you might want to explore in much greater detail?

This is a formative assessment strategy because it asks the learners to think about what they are doing, why they are doing it, and how it fits with the sequence of activity that they are undertaking.

A Spot of Theory

In Working Inside the Black Box, *Black et al (2004, p 11) note that:* 'Many teachers do not plan and conduct classroom dialogue in ways that might help students to learn'. *They recommend that talking with learners* '...can become part of the interactive dynamic of the classroom and can provide an invaluable opportunity to extend students' thinking through immediate feedback on their work'.

Use this to keep a record of what worked well for you and what didn't. A strategy that works with one class may not work so well with another. Keeping a checklist helps you to work out what factors or learner characteristics call for one approach rather than another. There's a line at the bottom for you to add your own most frequently used formative assessment strategy, if it's not already included in the list.

Strategy	Tried it with...	On...(date)	It worked	It didn't work	Worth trying again?
1. Listening in*					
2. Discussion, not monologue					
3. Traffic lights					
4. If I had five more minutes					
5. Why questions					
Your own strategy?					

DAY 2: What do you want them to learn?

In the most successful teaching, the focus of the planning is on successfully defining great learning, rather than being focused on the 'activities'. In other words, what you want learners to learn needs to be well thought out and defined, based on your knowledge of what learners have done and understood previously, what they perhaps haven't understood so well or haven't experienced yet and your in-depth knowledge of your learners. From this, a suitable learning sequence and activities can be defined. This gets you away from planning activities and then thinking, 'What did learners get from this?' They might actually be a very enjoyable set of activities but not have a particular learning focus or be of value.

It is not the case that the learning objectives need to be completely decided by you. Getting learners cognitively engaged in decisions about the learning can be extremely beneficial as it allows them ownership of the learning process. As well as involving them in the design of the curriculum, your learners' perceptions of the learning help you to understand their insider experience of the curriculum. You may even be surprised that your ideas of 'success' do not align with theirs.

This chapter puts learning at the heart of the work you are aiming to construct, and offers some practical ways for these important ideas to be realised, whether you are only just starting to plan your first lesson, or revising/constructing units of work as part of a curriculum. It takes you through a basic planning sequence and shows you how assessment is integral to the decisions made right from the outset. It gives you strategies for checking that learners understand what the desired learning is, and encourages you to explore ways to help you reflect on the lesson as it unfolds through the use of different types of assessment that will help hone your 'teacher radar'.

Today's strategies

1. Learning versus doing 1 – designing learning objectives

2. Learning versus doing 2 – what are they actually going to do?

3. Learners explaining aims – can they articulate what you want them to learn and do?

4. What do they think they know? / Finding out what they don't know

5. Planning time 1 – let them have time to plan before they actually start

6. Planning time 2 – reacting to formative assessment – how will you change what you are teaching as a result of knowing what they can/can't do?

7. Intentionality and purpose – do they know what they intend to do? Do they know what success looks like? Who decides? Sharing assessment criteria

Strategy: Learning versus doing 1 – designing learning objectives

Introduction

Planning the range of learning outcomes, rather than starting with the activities, really matters. Most likely, you will want to differentiate the learning, recognising that not all learners in the class are currently working from or to the same desired outcomes. The planning of the objectives is related to your assessment of where learners are currently at in their learning and where you want them to go next. The defined learning objectives need to be aspirational, suitably challenging and realistic. They also need to be easily understood and useful. In essence, the learning objectives are central to your own assessment of the success of a lesson or learning experience. In many cases you are not planning 'from scratch' because you will be basing your lessons broadly on a curriculum framework, which may be prescribed to a greater or lesser extent depending upon the context.

1. Learning versus doing 1

Think about the learning that you want to facilitate for a particular group of learners. Think about how this builds upon what they know/can do already and then think about 'where next?' In the early stages of teaching, it is likely that these learning objectives will be *instructional objectives* where desired learning is defined. When writing learning objectives, you need to be mindful of the following, based on your own varied assessment of the class. This may be based on what you have observed, examples of learners' work, the wider intentions of the unit, any other useful data you may have access to and your knowledge of the learners.

✺ What is it you want learners to learn in this lesson? This is not a list of 'knowledge' but instead defines what you want learners to know, understand and be able to do within this lesson.

✺ How does this relate to their current capabilities and prior experiences?

✺ Is it suitably aspirational and challenging for the group of learners you have in mind?

✺ Is it defined in language that learners will be able to understand?

Miss Mills is planning a science lesson for her Year 6 learners. They have been working on the unit *animals including humans*. Within the curriculum, one key aim is to *'recognise the impact of diet, exercise, drugs and lifestyle on the way their bodies function'* (DfE, 2015). The objective of this lesson is to explore one of these areas in more detail and to help children reflect upon the impact of diet. In the previous lesson learners explored the impact on the body of different types of exercise. Miss Mills defines two interlinked learning objectives for the lesson:

- to consider the positive and negative impacts of a diet;
- to use scientific evidence to identify healthy and unhealthy aspects of a diet.

Notice that this does not define the activities the class will undertake in order to do this but instead specifies the learning sought.

A Spot of Theory

There are different types of learning objectives, which guide learning in different ways. Over time, you will hopefully start to develop expressive objectives – a term coined by Eliot Eisner (1965). Instead of focusing on defining 'what' a learner will be able to do by the end of the lesson, expressive objectives encourage critical engagement and are much more open and flexible. An example of an expressive objective might be 'to develop a model using cardboard and glue' or 'to explore uses of magnets'.

Learning objectives

Strategy: Learning versus doing 2 – what are they actually going to do?

Introduction

Having defined the desired learning, you need to plan what learners are actually going to do in order to experience this learning. It is important that the learning is already defined before you select the activities that form the learning sequence, otherwise the activity may be a lot of fun but will not lead to the learning you have identified. Your 'assessment' of the success of the learning comes from whether, through doing the activities they are guided to do, learners have learned what you intended, however open this may be. Therefore, the activities should also be designed to allow learners to demonstrate what they have learned.

2. Learning versus doing 2

Once you have defined the learning objective, develop some activities and learning situations which lead to the development of the specified learning. Try to link up all of the activities in the lesson so that they work towards this defined objective or linked objectives – it is much easier for learners to make sense of the learning if there is an obvious link and it doesn't keep jumping from one thing to another. Think about the following questions.

- What is the learning objective?
- What do learners know and understand, and what are they able to do already?
- What misconceptions might they have?
- What are the best ways for this desired learning to be developed in this lesson?
- Will the activities and sequences of learning you have developed lead to this learning?
- How will you know? What are you looking for throughout the lesson in order to judge the relative success and guide/facilitate the learners as necessary?

Year 8 are exploring the use of moving images. So far in this unit, the learners have considered the development of the moving image, focusing on silent film and animation. This culminated in the class making their own flick books and scanning their pictures into the computer to be able to use again. The defined learning objective for today's work is *'to explore a mechanical means of animating images'*. Building on the previous work, Mr Douglas plans for the class to start designing and building their own zoetropes. In order to help them understand what a zoetrope is and what it is for, the starter activity demonstrates the use of a zoetrope and learners are encouraged to describe in their own words what it does and how it relates to other work in the unit. Groups of learners are given a zoetrope to look at and think about how it is constructed. They are given the following resources and set the task of creating their own, using the images scanned into the computer as the storyline.

- thin strips of white paper cut to size;
- thin strips of black paper cut to size;
- drawing materials;
- scissors;
- craft knives;
- cutting mats;
- cardboard lids;
- adhesive tape.

Mr Douglas observes the class as they work, que
to them as he goes round, making sure that the
the learning as they work towards making the
of the lesson he is able to judge, through a
content of the lesson meant that learners
a mechanical means of animating image

Strategy: Lea
articulate

Introduct

The purpos
of the a
their
to
us

A Spot of Theory

Smith et al (2005, p 115) note in their report, A Systematic Review of What Pupils, aged 11–16, Believe Impacts on their Motivation to Learn in the Classroom, *that* 'the way that assessment of the curriculum is constructed and practised in school appears to influence how learners see themselves as learners and social beings'. *It is important that learners are an integral factor in the construction of the curriculum and the assessment of it.*

...rners explaining aims – can they ...hat you want them to learn and do?

...ion

...ose of this strategy is for learners to share their understanding ...ms of the learning. This helps them to think about and articulate ...understanding of the learning in different ways and it helps you ...heck that their understanding aligns with what you intended. It is a ...eful strategy to implement before they start working on whatever you ...ave directed and also during the lesson when you interact with individual learners or groups.

3. Learners explaining aims

This strategy encourages learners to explain the aims of the learning to someone else – for example, to the teacher or to another group of learners. It is important not only for checking learners' understanding but also for keeping them on task and motivated within the lesson. It also helps them to articulate the purpose of the learning. Sometimes, as in the example below, it is useful to back up a verbal description of the aims with something practical. In other words, 'show me' as well as 'tell me'.

Acting as teacher to a group of peers

The Year 10 dance class are developing their understanding of embellishments through first-hand experience. Using a choice of three short routines with which the class are already familiar, they are set the task of being playful with the material and trying out embellishments, which Mrs Barre has already demonstrated and talked through with them. Before sending the class off to work in pairs on embellishment, Mrs Barre asks Darcey to explain what they are tasked with doing over the next six minutes.

Mrs Barre: *So, Darcey, can you explain the task to us please?*

Darcey: *We need to embellish our moves, Miss.*

Mrs Barre: *What does that mean?*

Darcey: *Er, to add some extra bits.*

Mrs Barre: *Thank you Darcey. Could you choose someone to show us how we might do this?*

Darcey: *Shakira.*

Mrs Barre: *Shakira, can you show us an example of embellishment? [Shakira demonstrates]*

Mrs Barre: *Thank you. Mikhail – why was that embellishment?*

Mikhail: *'Cos she added a hand movement, she sort of flicked it at the end.*

Mrs Barre: *Thank you, Mikhail. Why might this be useful please, Gary?*

Gary: *'Cos it makes the dance more complicated?*

Mrs Barre: *Sometimes, yes. Can anyone else help Gary with why we might use embellishment? Yes, Lizzy.*

Lizzy: *Because it makes the dance more interesting and it might help us to share the character with the audience.*

Mrs Barre: *Thank you Lizzy. Right, so you have six minutes to embellish the routine in any way you want. Have some fun with it!*

From this scenario, you can clearly see that by learners articulating what they need to do, they can communicate their understanding and you, as the teacher, have opportunities to make sure that the learning activity is serving its purpose.

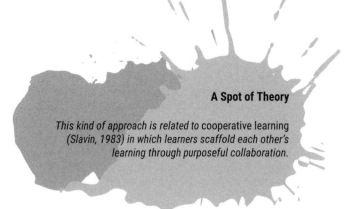

A Spot of Theory

This kind of approach is related to cooperative learning (Slavin, 1983) in which learners scaffold each other's learning through purposeful collaboration.

Strategy: What do they think they know? / Finding out what they don't know

Introduction

Learners already know stuff. A lot of stuff. And they also have things that they think they know, which might or might not be quite correct. Instead of thinking of learners as 'empty vessels' and assuming that you need to teach them from scratch, it is really important to find out what they do and don't know already. This does not need to be done as a test; there are loads of other creative ways to help you, and them, understand what they know already and therefore, what you might plan next in order to keep developing their learning.

4. What do they think they know? / Finding out what they don't know

Finding out what learners know is something you, as the teacher, always have your radar up for. We can learn a lot through listening to them talking and conversing with them, observing what they do and what they write and communicate through other media such as their artwork or audio recordings. The following strategy can be used at any point during the process to help guide the future decisions you make about the direction and focus of learning.

Ask learners to work together to create a 'thought shower' / 'spider diagram' about a particular topic, based on an open question. From what they write, and from listening to the discussions around the creation of this chart, the teacher is able to direct their questioning to probe further, and to unpack

any misconceptions or limitations in what learners know and understand already. This strategy is particularly useful at the beginning of a topic to avoid 'starting from scratch'. It can also be used at any point within a topic to consolidate learning. It doesn't even need to be a spider diagram; you could distribute a series of cards for learners to discuss or sort, or get them to design a quiz for other learners. The possibilities here are endless.

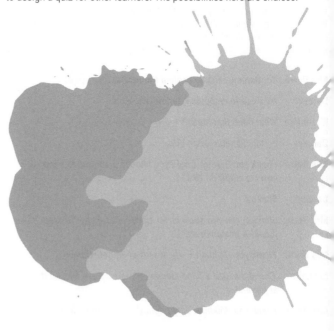

At the beginning of a music unit on reggae, Mrs Shaw wanted to know what learners know already. She set them the task of working in groups to design a thought shower to show *'everything you know about reggae music'*, having played *No Woman, No Cry* as the learners entered the room. In order to provide some scaffolding to get this started and avoid the potential for blank pieces of paper, she asked learners to generate one question to read out to the class, relating either to something they know about reggae music or something they might be interested to know. It could relate to any aspect – historical, social, cultural – or something about the music itself. The questions generated were very varied and included: *'Where in the world does it come from?'* and *'What makes it sound like reggae?'* The class shared their questions by reading them out loud, and were then given five minutes in groups of four to write down as many things as they could about reggae. While they were working, Mrs Shaw listened in to conversations and asked questions about what she heard in order to probe further and clarify information.

From eliciting this information, Mrs Shaw was able to adapt her planning so that she did not repeat what learners already knew. She was also able to open up a discussion on the historical roots of reggae music, and relate it to music from across time that the learners were already familiar with. Learner misconceptions, such as that the band *Madness* were a reggae band, were raised and Mrs Shaw was able to find ways to help learners differentiate between reggae and ska when playing and listening.

A Spot of Theory

As a teacher you have your radar up all the time, observing, listening and questioning. You see when someone looks nervous or looks at their feet when you ask the whole class a question, or when the task appears too easy or too difficult. You make instant adaptations based on all of these factors and so much more – as Swanwick (1999, p 71) notes, 'To teach is to assess'.

Strategy: Planning time 1 – let them have time to plan before they actually start

Introduction

In the real world, we spend time planning tasks before we undertake them. In the classroom, this very important step is often overlooked. The addition of structured planning time is beneficial at many points in the learning process. It is often beneficial that learners be given a few minutes to generate their ideas and, when working in groups, to discuss what they are going to do and how they might do it before they are set off to work independently on the task. For activities that run over from one lesson to another (as many do), introducing the planning time at the beginning of a subsequent lesson can help them to engage with the task from the previous week and work out what they might do next, ie setting themselves a work plan detailing how they might proceed. It is a very useful strategy to help you, as the teacher, be sure learners know what they are doing before setting off on a task, and to feed in ideas where necessary from listening in to what they say. It gives learners the confidence to generate ideas before they try them out.

5. Planning time 1

Explain to learners what they are aiming to do. Explain that they will have a limited amount of time (for example, six minutes) to plan out their ideas. Provide a structure for them to use if helpful. This may be a series of questions or a framework / set of prompt cards to help them think about what they are going to do.

The planning time may also be useful at other times during the process, for example, so that learners engage with feedback they have been given, and/ or their self-reflections. It can help them to refocus and move forward.

At the end of the lesson, reflect on the following questions:

- What did you notice about what they did during the planning time?
- What difference do you think it made to them as they worked through the rest of the task?
- Can you identify anything that you changed as a result of seeing, hearing or discussing with them during the planning time?
- What do you (and they) need to do next? How might this best happen?

Example 1

In drama, learners are working in groups to create their own script based around developing a short scene from a detective story. After dividing them into groups, Mr Peters sets the task, hands out pens and tells learners they have five minutes to plan a rough outline for the scene. He asks them to think about:

- What are the key events that happen in the scene?
- Who is in the scene? What character will each learner in the group take?
- What is their role?

While the learners are planning what to do, Mr Peters circulates the room and listens to the conversations, stopping by one of the tables to offer them some ideas when he overhears that they are stuck with generating their initial idea.

Example 2

At the beginning of the next drama lesson, each group is instructed to use tablet computers to watch the very short recording of their scene from the previous week, listen to the feedback which was recorded and work out what they are going to do in today's lesson to develop the characters and the plot further. Mr Peters tells learners that they have 10 minutes to watch, discuss and come up with the following to share with him before they start:

- at least two ideas to develop the plot;
- at least one way each in which they will develop their character.

As they discuss, Mr Peters listens in and asks questions or guides learners as required.

A Spot of Theory

Swanwick (1999, p 62) reminds us that 'assessing in everyday situations is often informal, intuitive'. *For teachers and practitioners, listening to learners talking and discussing together, sketching out and trying ideas, provides insightful evidence of their thinking, misconceptions and learning processes. This recognises the process of learning as being as valuable as the end product. The difficulty is that teachers frequently discredit this kind of intuitive 'assessment' because it is often not visible to others and does not 'measure' anything concrete. It is, however, vital.*

Strategy: Planning time 2 – reacting to formative assessment – how will you change what you are teaching as a result of knowing what they can/can't do?

Introduction

If you are intuitive in the classroom and use what you see and hear to constantly adapt your planning, then it is likely that you will lead more successful lessons. All the interactions you are involved in are based upon your assessment of what unfolds in the here-and-now. The questions you ask, the feedback you give and the direction in which you may guide learners or direct your lessons comes from this 'in the moment' assessment.

6. Planning time 2

By observing and listening to what is unfolding in the classroom, you are able to adapt what you do. This assessment of the situation guides what you do next. Have you assessed that someone is off task and needs refocusing? Have you been listening to their discussion and realised that they have some misunderstandings that need addressing? Have you gauged that they have no ideas to take their work forward and would benefit from some guidance? Have you observed that Gary has found the work too easy and needs a new challenge? Within a lesson, this reflection guides what you do next.

In exactly the same way, your planning of your next lesson should be based on all the information you have gleaned from the previous lesson, based on what you see and hear and the work produced and your knowledge of the class. By the end of the lesson, could the class do/know/understand what you wanted? If so, what next? If not, what do you need to do to help them move their learning forward? In other words, how will you change what you are teaching as a result of knowing what they can/can't do?

Providing guidance

In a mathematics investigation, the class have been split into groups to work out the answer to the question *'How big is Bigfoot?'* – to work out the area of a giant foot drawn on A1 paper (one drawing given to each group). From observing the class working on this in groups and talking to them, their teacher, Miss Patterson, realises that some groups have confused *perimeter* with *area*. In order to put this misconception right, she works with two small groups using drawings of a rectangle and then of a circle to help them to recognise the difference between perimeter and area and to develop some strategies that might help them to work out how to think about the area of Bigfoot. Before they go back to working on the area of Bigfoot, Miss Patterson helps them to recognise that they could split the foot into different sections to work out the overall area.

How big is Bigfoot?

A Spot of Theory

Assessment is not a bolt-on activity or something to be done at the end of an activity, but is integral to teaching and learning.

(Hickman, 2007, p 77)

Strategy: Intentionality and purpose – do they know what they intend to do?

Introduction

Given that each lesson lasts a finite period of time, you will have made some kind of plan to guide the learners within the session. Depending upon the given learning on any day, this might be done in a number of ways and be seeking many different outcomes. The intentions for the lesson may be quite specific or quite broad. Making sure that learners are aware of the broad intentions and the direction of travel is important, but this doesn't mean that the teacher needs to develop these and present them to learners as a 'done deal'. Giving learners opportunities to be involved in the development of what 'success' looks like is also useful.

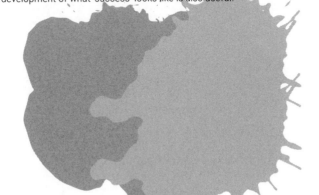

7. Intentionality and purpose

This strategy links to Strategy 1 from earlier in this chapter. Having decided the general direction of travel for the learning in the lesson, you need to think about how to communicate this to learners so that they are clear about what they are doing and why they are doing it. You need to decide what to share with learners – sometimes the learning is actually in the discovery of working out the point of the learning for themselves! Drawing this back together at the end of the lesson is important to help consolidate and deepen the learning.

You may also get learners to help you develop the assessment criteria themselves. This is often done through having shown various examples of what you are guiding the learners towards and asking them to come up with the success criteria. As well as giving you all something to 'judge' the work by throughout the process, this may provide a framework for helping learners to recognise the successes and shortfalls of their own work and provide some ideas for future development.

The Year 4 class are developing their own newspaper articles based on the story of an alien landing in their school playground. Having looked at various newspaper articles on recent stories and some exemplar work from last year, they discuss the ingredients of a really great article.

Mr Gregory: *OK – so you have two minutes to discuss with the person next to you what we might be looking for in a really great newspaper article and then we'll see if we can share some ideas.*

[2 minutes later] – Mr Gregory writes the suggestions on the flip chart.

Marcia: *It should be written in an exciting way that makes you think it's news.*

Kevin: *It needs a really punchy headline.*

Chris: *It needs to explain what happened.*

Paul: *It should have lots of facts and not the opinions of the reporter.*

Alan: *But it might have some words of what other people say describing what they saw or felt when they saw the aliens landing.*

Miranda: *It might have a photograph of the alien spaceship.*

Mr Gregory: *Is there anything else about the writing that is important?*

Marie: *It needs to be written in columns like you get in a newspaper.*

John: *It needs to have a hook like the one we looked at on the spaceman landing on the moon.*

Mr Gregory: *What about the sentences? Are these important?*

Ann: *Well it needs to be in full sentences and not in text speak. And it needs to have a short introduction.*

From going through this process, the learners have demonstrated that they know what they are aiming for, yet the content is relatively free. They will be able to use this list during the process to guide them and give them ideas, and to enable them to judge for themselves whether their work is effectively written in the style of a newspaper article.

Beyond this, each learner may well have individual targets they are working on, for example using speech marks appropriately, or starting sentences with a capital letter and ending with a full stop.

A Spot of Theory

Being involved in the development of the assessment criteria potentially offers learners ownership of the process, which can be important for motivation. These ideas of ownership have been developed over a long period of time and link to the notion of learners feeling autonomous in their learning as a strong motivational and self-determined process.

(Deci and Ryan, 1985)

If you only try one thing from this chapter, try this*

Use this to keep a record of what worked well for you and what didn't. A strategy that works with one class may not work so well with another. Keeping a checklist helps you to work out what factors or learner characteristics call for one approach rather than another. There's a line at the bottom for you to add your own most frequently used formative assessment strategy, if it's not already included in the list.

Strategy	Tried it with…	On…(date)	It worked	It didn't work	Worth trying again?
1. Learning vs doing 1					
2. Learning vs doing 2					
3. Learners explaining aims					
4. What do they think they know? / Finding out what they don't know*					
5. Planning time 1					
6. Planning time 2					
7. Intentionality and purpose					
Your own strategy?					

DAY 3: Tests and quizzes in the classroom

When we think about tests, we probably immediately think about 'exams' and high-stakes tests. Yet, we test learners all the time; we ask questions to test understanding, to unearth misconceptions and for so many other reasons that could loosely be defined as 'testing'. Tests and quizzes do not need to be written – there are many examples where we test learners through discussion and presentation. Likewise with quizzes – do we immediately think of word searches? Game shows? Pub quizzes of declarative memorised knowledge?

This chapter adopts the approach of using tests and quizzes to help consolidate and extend learning. It considers the skills teachers need in order to make tests and quizzes effective. This links to the types of questions we ask and how we ask them. It also considers how to construct reliable and valid summative assessments. Reliability considers the trustworthiness of the measure or outcome, whereas validity refers to the credibility of the outcome. It is in this context that this chapter is constructed; to help you design effective assessment tools that are useful and meaningful.

1. Question stems – Bloom's taxonomy and question types

2. Wait time / no hands up – try giving thinking time

3. Keep it going – don't just take the first answer, keep going to get more detail and information

4. Validity and reliability: using data – look at data and evidence you have on learners, what it does and doesn't tell you. Are you just assessing their use of English – how do you know?

5. Short-term memory aided by quizzes – repetition, spiral curriculum, moving from short-term to long-term memory, chunking

6. Learners write questions – these may be for the rest of the class

Strategy: Question stems – Bloom's taxonomy and question types

Introduction

Planning for questioning is an important part of a teacher's armoury. While we ask many questions spontaneously, the best questions are asked after those which have been thought out in advance and which open up thinking. Simply put, questions are described as *closed* if they have one answer, often based on recall of facts, or *open* if they require a deeper level of thinking and may give rise to different responses.

Bloom's Taxonomy (1956) is an often-cited hierarchical framework for developing increasingly higher-order thinking. Probably the most significant development of this came from Anderson and Krathwohl (2001). Using these hierarchical thinking frameworks as a basis for questioning leads to the possibility of asking questions that require a greater level of cognitive engagement and go beyond the simple 'yes/no' questions that may come from unplanned questions.

1. Question stems

Using question stems relating to the taxonomy can be helpful for planning differentiated questions in advance, and to help learners more fully explore and engage with a topic. Examples of question stems using the different categories are shown below. These move away from simple recall of factual knowledge. Questions can be sequenced to move from lower-order to higher-order thinking, from recall to creating new knowledge.

Question stems derived from Bloom's Taxonomy

Knowledge/remembering	Can you tell me what you are doing?
Comprehension/understanding	Can you explain to me how you are doing it?
Application/applying	How will you do this?
Analysis/analysing	Can you explain to me why you are doing it?
Synthesis	How might you do it differently?
Evaluation/evaluating	Do you think this was successful?
Creating	Can you produce a solution?

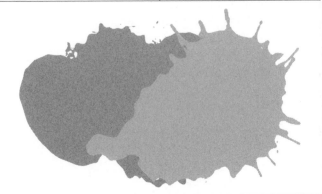

Year 3 are carrying out a science experiment using magnets. In order to check and develop their understanding, Miss Green questions them as she moves from group to group. Moving to the second group, she stops and converses.

Miss Green: *Can you show me what you are doing?*

Sue: *Well, we're trying to work out if these different things are magnetic or not. [Points to the box of objects.]*

Miss Green: *So can you explain how you are doing that?*

Steve: *Well, we're holding the magnet near the object and it picks up the object that is magnetic and they stick together.*

Miss Green: *OK, so is there anything in particular about the objects that it picks up? Compare these with those it doesn't pick up. What do you notice?*

Olivya: *It only picks up the shiny ones.*

Miss Green: *What do you mean by shiny? Is there anything else you notice? Take a look at the pile of things that you have identified as magnetic.*

Olivya: *Well, they've all got a bit of metal on them.*

Miss Green: *What do you predict will happen if you put one magnet near the other one?*

Andy: *I think it will pick it up because it's metal.*

Miss Green: *OK, do you predict it will pick up any part of the magnet? And give me a reason for your answer. I'll be back in two minutes, after you've discussed it. And then I'll give you another magnet and you can try it out.*

In this conversation, Miss Green carefully scaffolded the conversation through increasingly high-order questioning to help learners think about what had happened in the experiment and why, moving them towards predicting what might happen in different situations, in order to help them understand magnetism and how it works.

A Spot of Theory

Learning can be considered as the process by which people acquire, understand, apply and extend knowledge, concepts, skills and attitudes. Children and young people also discover their feelings towards each other and towards learning itself… The teachers' recognition of what learners bring to their education is crucial.

(Pollard et al, 2014, p 34)

Strategy: Wait time / no hands up – try giving thinking time

Introduction

Often when we question learners, we ask a question and expect an immediate response. Ideally, though, we need to provide a framework for learners to be able to understand the question and have time to formulate a considered response in more detail, rather than blurting out the first thing that comes into their head. This means providing time between a question being asked and a response being expected.

2. Wait times / no hands up

In effect, we have two strategies rolled into one here. The first – wait time – means that, after asking a question, you will wait a period of time before expecting a response. Even 30 seconds seems like a long time to wait in a classroom but it is worth it so that everyone gets to formulate a response and to develop this response. The second part of this strategy – no hands up – gets learners away from thinking that they need to put their hand up immediately after you have finished asking a question (or before!) and encourages them to formulate a response before answering. By waiting for a short period of time and keeping their hands down, everyone has an incentive to do the thinking for themselves, rather than the same few learners always putting their hands up.

Applying the 'no hands up' strategy

In the Year 6 mathematics lesson the class have been working on multiplication, with learners working through differentiated examples. At the end of the lesson, Mrs Shepherd wants to check their understanding of the term *multiplication* and how it works. This question is at the start of the plenary.

Mrs Shepherd:

" *I would like you to think about how you would explain multiplication to someone else. Imagine that when you get to Grandma's house she asks what you have been doing at school this week and you say 'multiplication'. If she says ' what does that mean?' how would you explain it? I'm going to give you 30 seconds to think up your response, so don't put your hands up, just think about your answer. So, think on your own for 30 seconds about how you would explain multiplication clearly.*

Mrs Shepherd waits 30 seconds and the question, *'How would you explain multiplication?'* is also shown on the board during that time. At the end of this time she turns to the class and says:

" *Ok, I want you to explain what multiplication is to the person next to you, and then I will choose someone to share their explanation with the whole class.*

In this example, the teacher has set a question needing time and consideration and given the class time to think it through and therefore cognitively engage with the question.

A Spot of Theory

It is recognized that the effect of the teacher creating a wait time (approximately 3–5 seconds) before taking an answer has a significant impact upon increasing learning as the number of learners engaged in thinking hopefully increases as well as the quality of the answer improving.

(Spendlove, 2009, p 40)

Strategy: Keep it going – don't just take the first answer, keep going to get more detail and information

Introduction

Sometimes it is useful to bounce a question round to different learners in order to get more detail, to clarify points and to keep everyone involved. A real advantage of this strategy is that questions can be carefully differentiated and responses can be scaffolded in order to support all learners to contribute and to feel confident to try out their answers even when they are not 100 per cent sure they are correct. As with all questioning, the teacher may find it useful to plan some of the questions in advance so that they can be targeted to particular learners and therefore be appropriately challenging.

3. Keep it going

The way in which this strategy works is usually for the teacher to ask the first question and, following wait time, choose a learner to answer or respond to the question asked. Other learners may then be invited to comment on the response, extend the response, disagree with the response, add detail to the response or bring in other points or opinions. For the final bounce of the question, one learner may be selected to consolidate all of the information gleaned from other learners and asked to summarise this back to the rest of the class in order to provide a more detailed response to the original question.

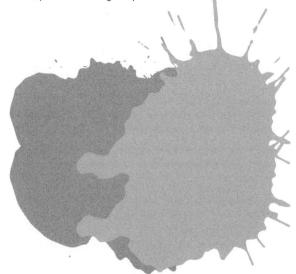

The English A level class are working on persuasive writing.

Mrs Stevenson: *So, before we start writing our own persuasive writing pieces, let's just have a quick think about ways the blogger used to persuade the reader in the example we read together. Have a think on your own and then I will ask someone. [Waits 30 seconds.] Dan – give me one of the ways.*

Dan: *They included facts about people's use of technology.*

Mrs Stevenson: *Thanks Dan. Katie, can you give an example of any of the facts?*

Katie: *That more people are accessing the internet on their mobile phones.*

Mrs Stevenson: *And are those kinds of facts good to use, Greg?*

Greg: *Yes.*

Mrs Stevenson: *Why do you think that, Greg?*

Greg: *Because they come from credible sources. Whereas if they couldn't back up what they were saying or used something that doesn't sound official we might not believe it.*

Mrs Stevenson: *What else is important, Ella?*

Ella: *That they have a very clear argument and know what they want readers to think.*

Mrs Stevenson: *Andy – can you add to that?*

Andy: *Well, the language they use is very persuasive. They give a lot of reasons why banning technology in classrooms is a really bad idea and link it with lots of different ideas. And the sentence structure – it started with a really short sentence.*

Mrs Stevenson: *OK, so Rita, can you give us the main thing you are really trying to do in your own persuasive writing?*

Rita: *To persuade the reader to agree with what I am saying and make it sound credible and interesting.*

A Spot of Theory

Black and Wiliam's seminal work, Inside the Black Box *(1998), notes that the quality of questioning is a fundamental driver to raising understanding.*

Strategy: Validity and reliability – look at data and evidence you have on learners, what it does and doesn't tell you. Are you just assessing their use of English – how do you know?

In any school there is data about learners that teachers have access to and also generate through their teaching. Some of this data is potentially more useful than other data, but ultimately you need to think about what you want to achieve and how useful data may or may not be in that particular context or situation.

Validity and reliability are terms you may come across when discussing assessment in your context. Each has a specific meaning.

❋ *Validity*, in essence, refers to whether the assessment is actually assessing what it is supposed to be assessing, or something else entirely. We will address this again later when we discuss construct-irrelevant assessment. Put crudely, does the assessment assess the topic in hand, or does it *actually* assess, say, use of written English in being able to write up the assessment?

❋ *Reliability* refers to whether the data from an assessment is repeatable in terms of, say, the same assessment being marked and graded by a different teacher, or a different group of learners of similar abilities getting the same grades if they did the same task. It can also refer to whether learners would obtain the same outcome if they undertook the task on a different occasion.

When you use tests devised by external agencies, they have hopefully been thought about in terms of their reliability and validity. If you are constructing your own, you may want to give some thought as to whether your tests are valid, and whether your grading (if you are doing it yourself) is reliable!

4. Validity and reliability: using data

Reflecting

When thinking about the relative success of learning through a lesson you have taught, you may use a variety of data to help form your judgements. For example, when looking through test scores from an end-of-unit test, you can think about which areas of learning are generally secure and which need more work. You can also identify learners who need a greater level of challenge and those who may need more support. You also need to reflect upon whether the test data, which you are basing these judgements on, was fit for purpose in this context. For example, did the questions you asked contribute to your learning intentions? If everybody in the class scored lower than you expected on a particular aspect, what do you need to do in your teaching to remedy this situation? What else do you know about these learners from other data about their learning and situation that would help you make sense of what they did and what you observed? How might you use that more effectively in the future?

Planning

As a teacher you need to plan learning experiences relating to what has gone before. Having reflected on previous learning and used appropriate and wide-ranging data to support these reflections, you can plan the next steps. The planning and the use of data are integrally related to the learning intentions. Having identified these and made sure that they are appropriate for the wide range of learners in the class, you can use the data to design learning.

Mr Newton teaches chemistry in a secondary school. He has devised an experiment using scientific apparatus, which the Year 10 learners have to assemble, and then follow instructions carefully to dissolve two substances in a liquid, and then heat it. Having completed the experiment, the learners are required to write up what they did, under three headings: apparatus/method/results.

Mr Newton has being doing this work and its associated assessment for a few years now, and one day his head of science, Cathy, comes to see him:

Cathy: *Hi Dave, I've been looking at the results from your latest assessments, and I noticed something interesting.*

Dave: *Oh, what's that?*

Cathy: *Your chemistry grades are almost the same as the grades those Year 10s got in their last English assessment, when we compared them at the leadership meeting.*

Dave: *Oh, why is that interesting?*

Cathy: *Because, they are more similar to their English grades than anything else from science.*

Dave and Cathy talk about this for a while, and it dawns on Dave that what he has actually been grading is his Year 10s' use of English. In order to investigate this further, Cathy comes and talks to his Year 10s, and finds they do understand what the experiment was all about, but that some simply hadn't described it as well as those whose use of English was of a high standard. He wasn't marking their scientific knowledge; he was marking their use of English.

This was not, Dave and Cathy concluded, a very valid form of assessment!

A Spot of Theory

Gordon Stobart notes that:

Validity is not a static property of a test, something it has or does not have, but is contingent on what a test is for, how it is used, and how the results are interpreted. Validity is about purposes and uses as well as about what is in the test.

(Stobart, 2009, p 162)

Strategy: Short-term memory aided by quizzes – repetition, spiral curriculum, moving from short-term to long-term memory, chunking

Introduction

While the aim of education is to promote in-depth thinking and committing understanding to long-term memory, there is a place for developing short-term memory in order to aid this. Quizzes can be a great way to do this. The important thing is that the quiz design and questions should support the planned learning. There are many different ways to put together a quiz – if you search online, you will find templates for many different quiz shows in which you can include your own questions. Quizzes could be completed individually, but they also lend themselves well to being tackled in teams. They could be timed; they could be more open. You might even consider letting learners design their own quizzes and set challenges for each other, so long as the learning parameters are made clear.

5. Short-term memory aided by quizzes

Once you have defined what it is you want learners to know, understand and be able to do, you might want to design a quiz. This may be used to:

- find out what they don't know;
- help them to remember;
- consolidate learning.

Decide on the best format of a quiz for this purpose. Will it be online? Through completion of a sheet? Through discussion? Through playing a game?

Find a way to set questions for the quiz that are directly linked to the learning. How will you know they know? Yes/no questions allow a 50 per cent chance of guessing the right answer, and likewise multiple-choice questions involve some element of chance, so you may want to minimise these. Earlier in this chapter you had an opportunity to explore question types in more detail; think about how you can incorporate these into the quiz.

How will the quiz be marked? Online? By you? By the class? How will the 'scoring' work? Quizzes can make learners quite competitive and so you need to ensure that marks are fairly awarded (for example, two marks for a completely correct response, one mark for a mostly correct response).

Finally, you need to look through the quiz and check that learners will understand why they have done something; sometimes in a quiz the point of the learning can be lost.

Mr Rodrigues wants to check Year 5 learners' basic understanding of the Tudor period and to help them commit some ideas about the Tudor period to memory. This is their third lesson on the Tudor period. He writes a list of basic things that he wants learners to know:

- the relationship between Henry VIII and previous/next kings or queens;
- how ascension to the throne happened;
- when the Tudors reigned and what came before/after;
- the names of the wives and children of Henry VIII;
- how separation from the Pope came about, and the impact on religion in England;
- England's relationship with Europe.

The quiz is designed in a booklet for learners to complete in teams of three. He designs the questions around these points, using a combination of:

- multiple-choice questions;
- short-answer one-line responses;
- putting possible answers in the right sequence;
- ticking the 'fake news';
- questions requiring three bullet points to answer.

Each group was given 20 minutes to complete the quiz and also to write one quiz question for the other groups to answer. In order to complete the quiz, learners were given access to their notes from previous lessons and an online history resource site. At the end of the 20 minutes, the class swapped booklets and they went through the quiz answers.

A Spot of Theory

Metacognition (sometimes called learning to learn*) can have a significant impact on a learner's outcomes. As the Education Endowment Fund have noted in their studies:* 'These strategies are usually more effective when taught in collaborative groups so learners can support each other and make their thinking explicit through discussion' *(EEF, 2017).*

Strategy: Learners write questions – these may be for the rest of the class

Introduction

If learners were to ask the questions about something, what would they ask? Often the questions they ask are far more sophisticated than what we might think they will come up with. Giving learners a framework to ask questions also encourages them to think about the learning in different ways and to give them ownership of the learning process. Additionally, the questions they ask give us an insight into how they are thinking about something, and sometimes also highlight misconceptions they may have. Remember that much of the learning here is in the composing of the questions, as well as what you may do with them afterwards. There is not necessarily a need for the questions – or the answers – to be written down.

6. Learners write questions

There are many ways of encouraging learners to write questions. Here are just two examples, but by using your imagination, you are bound to come up with others.

A. In order to consolidate learning, instead of writing questions yourself, ask learners to write the questions for each other. Make sure that they are sure about what they need to check that each other knows and understands, and construct the questions accordingly. You will need to give them guidance as to the style of questions they could use, which may be differentiated so that this is focused and directed for the learner writing the question (eg multiple-choice, short-answer, exploratory, analytical, probing).

B. You could provide question stems to encourage learners to ask a range of questions. One way to do this is to ask learners to think of a question starting with a given word or phrase and write it down. They fold over the top of the paper so the question can't be seen, and then the question paper is passed to the person on their left. This continues with increasingly higher-order question openings being asked so that a few different questions are generated, each by a different person. After the final question is generated, the papers are moved on again and then opened, with the questions and possible responses being shared through discussion with a small group.

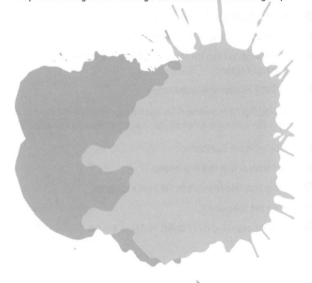

A. In a GCSE English class, the learners are close to taking their final examination. Instead of being given short-answer questions to respond to about a specific set text, the learners are encouraged to write three potential questions of their own and to swap them with another learner.

B. In order to generate a discussion around a piece of artwork by Giuseppe Arcimboldo, Year 7 learners are encouraged to write interesting questions for discussion. A copy of the painting is shown on the interactive whiteboard.

Each piece of paper is folded over and passed on after each question. Learners write questions with the following openings:

- What...
- How...
- Why...
- Compare...
- Justify...

Following this, learners are split into groups of four to discuss the questions and their ideas about the possible responses from their own perspective.

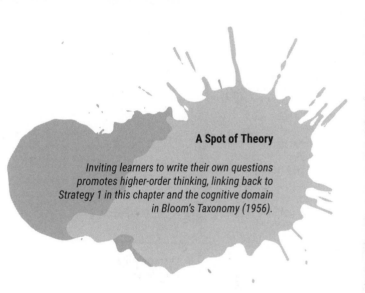

A Spot of Theory

Inviting learners to write their own questions promotes higher-order thinking, linking back to Strategy 1 in this chapter and the cognitive domain in Bloom's Taxonomy (1956).

If you only try one thing from this chapter, try this*

Use this to keep a record of what worked well for you and what didn't. A strategy that works with one class may not work so well with another. Keeping a checklist helps you to work out what factors or learner characteristics call for one approach rather than another. There's a line at the bottom for you to add your own most frequently used formative assessment strategy, if it's not already included in the list.

Strategy	Tried it with...	On...(date)	It worked	It didn't work	Worth trying again?
1. Question stems					
2. Wait time / no hands up					
3. Keep it going					
4. Validity and reliability: using data					
5. Short-term memory aided by quizzes					
6. Learners write questions*					
Your own strategy?					

DAY 4: Who is the assessment for?

Assessment is really important, and so today's chapter focuses on thinking about who is it important *for*. You can think about assessment data as having a number of audiences. At its most straightforward these include:

- you, the teacher;
- the learners you teach;
- parents/carers;
- school systems, including the headteacher and Senior Leadership Team (SLT).

If you consider each of these audiences, and what they might want from the assessment data you produce, you will find some different but overlapping requirements. Put simply these are as follows:

- Teacher: How are the learners doing? What do I need to go over again? What can we move on to next? Who is ready to move on? How well do they know the topic? How well have I taught it and what might I do differently next time? Have they made sufficient progress?

- Learners: How am I doing? Have I done as well as my mates? Do I understand this topic? Are there bits I'm not sure about? Do I think I've done as well as I could have done? What do I need to do better at in future?

- Parents/carers: How well is she or he doing? Are they happy in class? Are they enjoying this topic? How has she or he done compared with the rest of the class? Is there anything I can do to help with this in future?

- School systems: What are the grades for this class? Have they made sufficient progress? How has this teacher's class done compared with the others? Is the class on-target for future grades in external exams/tests? Does this teacher need an intervention strategy?

All of these are important uses and purposes for assessment, but a key question for the busy classroom is often *'Can one assessment do all this?'*

Today's strategies

- Holistic assessment versus assessment moments
  1. Holistic assessment
  2. Assessment moments

- What is being assessed?
  3. Attainment and/or achievement?
  4. Assessment for progression

- Grades, comments, or both?
  5. Grades – up and down?
  6. Comments, and comment-only marking

- What do parents need to know?
  7. Reporting – how they are doing
  8. Reporting – attitude and effort

Strategy: Holistic assessment versus assessment moments

Introduction

It is important to be clear here on the differences between formative and summative assessment. We have seen how it is often true that formative assessment makes the most difference to learning, so in this strategy we want you to think about the different ways you think about assessment with your learners. Holistic assessment can take many forms, but for today, let's think about this as being when you give a grade (so summative assessment) for a learner's overall performance throughout a topic. Assessment moments are when you intervene with formative assessments, and award summative grades for aspects of learner performance as they go along. The nature of the topic you are teaching, or maybe the subject as a whole, will also have a part to play in determining whether you use holistic assessment, or go for assessment moments. It may also be the case that you change during the course of a unit of work, and swap over.

There is no right way of doing this! One will be appropriate on some occasions, and the other at different times. Your school policy will also affect how you do this. Some schools *only* permit work recorded in the 'assessment lesson' to count for grading. Others permit teachers to work in any way which suits them. What is the policy at your school?

1. Holistic assessment

Holistic assessment involves you awarding a grade at the end of a scheme, unit or other significant point. To do this, you can use awarding criteria or comparative judgement; or – what some teachers simply rely on – a 'feeling' for how a learner has performed on a piece of work or, say, in a portfolio of evidence.

2. Assessment moments

Assessment moments can be put into place for any work that you are doing with your learners. For some, this will be a specific piece of writing; for others, a moment which involves doing something which is graded. Some teachers talk of 'catching them doing well', and breaking learning down into a series of tasks, which they then grade as the work is in process.

Assessment moments have a built-in advantage of being able to afford you and the learners a snapshot of how they are doing at that particular time, on that specific task. It may well be the case that you use assessment moments in order to see if the class have grasped an important aspect of the topic in hand before you and they move on to what is coming next. Some teachers talk of *threshold concepts*, key points which need to be grasped for effective learning to take place. Assessment moments enable you to get a feeling for this with your learners.

Mrs Chants, a secondary-school music teacher, is teaching a unit of work on songwriting to her Year 9 class. In the past she has always used an assessment lesson to give a grade to her learners, but now her school has changed its assessment policy, she no longer needs to do this. What she decides to do instead is to trial using holistic assessment, for which she will give a mark out of 20 (this is a school policy) for each learner's work over the course of the songwriting unit.

This unit takes six weeks to complete, with one lesson per week, and involves a fair amount of learner autonomy. However, throughout the unit she gives the learners the opportunity to perform their songs, either to small groups of their friends, or to the whole class. As she goes from learner to learner discussing their work with them – in other words, undertaking formative assessment – she asks the learners to make a note of their conversations. She looks over these notes during her lessons with the class over the six-week period. The only stipulation Mrs Chants has is that the song must be recorded. She doesn't mind if they do this at home on their phones, or in school.

At the end of the unit she has heard all the songs, read all the formative assessment conversations, and awarded marks out of 20 to each learner.

● Read the Spot of Theory feature opposite. Do you agree with Sadler's views about holistic assessment?

A Spot of Theory

Sadler observes:

...the unique value of holistic judgements needs to be appreciated, with openness to incorporating criteria that are not on a fixed list. To maintain technical and personal integrity, a number of significant shifts in the assessment environment are necessary. The commitment to mechanistic use of preset criteria needs to be abandoned.

(Sadler, 2010, p 62)

Strategy: What is being assessed?

To know what you are assessing may seem an obvious starting point, but sometimes it turns out not to be that obvious after all! Let's dig a little deeper today...

3. Attainment and/or achievement?

These two words are very similar, but actually have different meanings. *Attainment* is concerned with the actual marks or grades a learner has been awarded in summative assessments. Ofsted look at '*...pupils' academic achievement over time, taking attainment and progress into account*' (Ofsted, 2012, p 8). *Achievement* is more concerned with distance travelled, in assessment terms, and how taxing this has been for the individual. For example, an outstanding athlete may come top in running the 100 metres, but this is not much of an achievement; a reluctant runner may break their own record, they may come last, but they have achieved an improvement. Graded solely on time, learner 1 has better attainment, but learner 2 may have actually achieved more. Complicated, isn't it!

Here are some of the differences between the two.

Attainment	Achievement
Marks for a single instance	Change in marks over time
Measured by a single summative assessment	Measured over a series of summative assessments
Involves no view of progression	Builds into a view of progression

These lists are not exhaustive. What else might you add to them, and what else do you need to know to make a judgement about achievement?

4. Assessment for progression

Progression is all about getting from one place in learning to another. We talk of learners making 'rapid' or 'slow' progress, as there is an element of speed involved too. Assessment for progression takes into account a number of factors:

* cumulative grades from a series of summative assessments;
* speed at which a learner moves through these;
* knowledge of where a learner is at now;
* knowledge of where that learner can be encouraged to get to next;
* formative assessment comments aimed at developing attainment;
* taking a series of summative assessments over a period of time to judge speed.

Lots of these progression assessments involve journey words – *speed, movement, location, direction*. In making your teacher assessments you will need to be aware of these, and you will need to know your learners, as you will want to maximise their opportunities to make good progress. You will often meet learners who are just 'coasting'; they need attention to ensure that they maximise their learning opportunities.

As you prepare your next summative assessments, think about these three words – *attainment, achievement* and *progression*. Ask yourself what you are intending to assess, and what will happen to this data. Is it to help the learners? We would hope so – but is it also being used to assess your teaching? Is it being used to compare learners?

Think of a unit of work you will be teaching soon. Ask yourself these questions:

1. What am I assessing?
2. Who are the assessment results intended for: learners, me, school systems, parents?
3. What form will the assessment take?

These are all general questions, so now let's drill down a little further:

4. How might you calculate attainment and achievement separately for your learners?
5. How might you assess progress?

Let's try and think of some answers teachers might give to the last two questions now. Which, if any, of the following would you agree with?

4: A. I don't bother with achievement, I just give them all a test.

B. I know my learners, and I have an expected grade in mind. If they do better, they have achieved well; if worse, they have not achieved well.

C. I average all of my class's scores, and compare them with each other to see who comes out best.

5: D. I add up each learner's individual scores, and average them to see if they are beating their own average.

E. I expect them to get gradually better marks during the year.

Thoughts? Well, point a) seems a little reductive. Point b) seems to be similar to point d), but involving less statistical analysis. Point c) may prove useful, but care needs to be taken as the results of a few learners could skew things for the majority. Point d) is a form of ipsative assessment, and again, may prove useful, but for a busy teacher point b) may be sufficient. Point e) relies on you being consistent in your marking, and the assessments to be consistent in their difficulty. This is quite hard to achieve!

✸ Can you improve on these answers? What ideas do you have for assessing attainment, achievement and progression?

A Spot of Theory

There are several potential advantages in using teachers' judgements more widely as part of summative assessment for external as well as internal uses. First, teachers are making judgments about students' attainment in the course of their normal interactions during teaching and learning. Second, in this process teachers can build up a picture of students' attainments across the full range of activities and goals.

(Harlen, 2005, p 212)

Strategy: Grades, comments, or both?

As you have seen, formative assessment is often best thought of as being in conversational style, and is unlikely to involve a grade or mark. But summative assessment does involve grading and marking, and there are three likely forms this can take:

- only a grade;
- a grade and a comment;
- only a comment.

Each of these has a number of connotations, so let us think about them.

5. Grades – up and down?

Grading work is an essential component of summative assessment. This seems non-contentious, but some teachers have a problem with their school's policy. This is because in some schools teachers are *not allowed* to give learners a lower grade than the one they achieved previously. This was common in the days of national curriculum levels, when subdivided levels meant that a learner awarded a Level 4c could only be awarded a Level 4b next time, or else the teacher would be in trouble! Some schools have continued with this policy; it is known as unilinear grading, meaning grades can only go up. Is this the policy in your school?

6. Comments, and comment-only marking

For many learners, the grade on a piece of work is all they will look at, or care about. As Gordon Stobart notes, '...*evidence suggests that accompanying comments are largely ignored; it is the grade that matters*' (Stobart, 2008, p 167). What this means is that however much work you put into writing helpful comments on a piece of written work, in many cases this will make very little difference to the learners. One way of addressing this issue is used in some schools, and this is *comment-only marking*. What happens here is exactly as the name implies: you mark work with a comment only. You can add a grade if you wish, but you do not do so on the learner's work itself; you record this for your own purposes in your own mark book.

Using comment-only marking, however, does take some educating of the learners (and their parents!) as they will be used to comparing marks. We know that this can upset high-attaining learners, as they like their high grades as affirmation.

Mr Wright is a geography teacher in a secondary school which has recently introduced comment-only marking. He is finding that the job of marking homework has been speeded up by this, as he always used to mark points of improvement for the learners in his classes, but now he does not have to agonise over whether this is a Level 5b or a Level 5c assignment, as his school has also abandoned levels. This means his learners are now reading his comments, and, what is more, actually acting on them the next time they have an assignment. This is a real change!

What Mr Wright has found, though, is that he tends to write a lot of similar comments for many learners; so the geography department has developed a shorthand code for all the teachers, and the learners have a copy too. This means Mr Wright can concentrate on matters of substance, ones which make a difference to learning.

A Spot of Theory

All quarter long papers would go back to the students with comments but no grades, although the grades were entered in a book. … Then a hoped-for phenomenon began. During the third or fourth week some of the A students began to get nervous and started to turn in superb work and hang around after class with questions that fished for some indication as to how they were doing. The B and high-C students began to notice this and work a little and bring up the quality of their papers to a more usual level. The low C, D and future F's began to show up for class just to see what was going on…

(Pirsig, 1974, p 202)

Strategy: What do parents need to know?

Reporting to parents is an important part of the cycle of work that a school does. However, it is all too easy to bombard parents with information which may not necessarily be helpful to them. As it is assessment data which will, by-and-large, form the basis of what you tell parents, it is worth spending some time thinking about this.

7. Reporting – how they are doing

An obvious thing to report to parents is how their children are getting on academically. This will take the form of reporting on test scores and exam results, but it is worth reflecting on whether you think this is telling the whole story. Attainment grades alone may not be all the information that you wish to convey to parents, nor might it be all that a parent wishes to hear, or needs to know. Is there a story behind the grades? What else is going on? What is that learner like in your classroom?

8. Reporting – attitude and effort

Grading attainment is often fairly straightforward – it is often the results which you already have in your mark book; grading attitude or effort is often somewhat harder as it requires you to really think about what grade you will put on this. Some schools do not use effort or attitude grades at all, so it may not be something you have had to think much about. Is yours like this?

Even if it isn't, you may want to think about using these grades in class, and for reporting to parents. If you have learners who really try hard, and seem to do their best, but their attainment is always outshone by other learners, then maybe you want to reward these learners? Attitude and effort grades are the way to do it. Even though they are subjective, they can still mean a lot to the learners.

Ask yourself these questions:

- Who has tried the hardest?
- Who has attained the most? And the least?
- Is there a link between attainment and effort? Have some learners simply 'sailed through' and others had to put more into it?

Sometimes doing this lets you see your learners in a whole new light!

Seeing your learners in a whole new light

Miss Baker teaches a Year 5 primary school class. She has some learners who always attain high grades, and she knows that one boy, Damien, can score well on tests with ease, but his written work is often rushed. She is concerned that other harder-working learners are getting disheartened, so she introduces effort grades to her Year 5s, as well as the customary attainment grades. Damien does not score so highly on this.

Put yourself in Miss Baker's position. How will you deal with Damien's dissatisfaction? Kamaljit, on the other hand, is delighted. She always tries hard, but does not score as well as Damien. How will you deal with this? What will you want to report to parents?

Here is what Miss Baker said:

Miss Baker: *Damien, I know you are disappointed with your effort grade, but your attainment grade hasn't altered from your usual ones. How long did it take you to do this work?*

Damien: *About 10 minutes, Miss.*

Miss Baker: *I see. What would it have been like if you'd spent, say, 20 minutes on it?*

Damien: *I don't know Miss, I just like to get it finished!*

Miss Baker: *Yes, but that is why your effort grade is not as high as some other learners. They have spent more time, and importantly, taken more care with their presentation. Do you think you could do that next time please, Damien?*

Kamaljit: *Miss, it took me ages, and I still haven't done as well as Damien!*

Miss Baker: *Kamaljit, you have a higher effort grade. That's why I've introduced them, to show that your work is very neat, and pleasing to look at. You should be pleased!*

Kamaljit: *I am, Miss, just checking!*

A Spot of Theory

Reporting test performance ... obscures some important information, exaggerates the importance of other information, and can provide a seriously distorted view of differences and trends.

(Koretz, 2009, p 183)

Checklist

Use this to keep a record of what worked well for you and what didn't. A strategy that works with one class may not work so well with another. Keeping a checklist helps you to work out what factors or learner characteristics call for one approach rather than another. There's a line at the bottom for you to add your own most frequently used strategy, if it's not already included in the list.

Strategy	Tried it with…	On…(date)	It worked	It didn't work	Worth trying again?
1. Holistic assessment					
2. Assessment moments					
3. Attainment and/or achievement					
4. Assessment for progression					
5. Grades – up and down?					
6. Comments, and comment-only marking*					
7. Reporting – how are they doing?					
8. Reporting – attitude and effort					
Your own strategy?					

DAY 5: Using assessment to improve learning

Introduction

Assessing progress and attainment of learners is clearly important; but having done this, you also need to do something with the information that your assessments, whether formative or summative, yield. This information is referred to as *assessment data*. It is important that you do not just think of assessment data as being numbers, grades or levels – in other words, things that can be entered into a spreadsheet; assessment data also includes results from formative assessment conversations, and from the other strategies discussed on Day 1. Having obtained all this rich assessment data, today's strategies focus on what you do with it in order to make your teaching and learning more meaningful.

It is worthwhile to note that the assessment data you have produced can influence your teaching in a number of ways, from thinking about how to plan for learning, to how to teach with specific learners in mind. Assessment data, as you have seen, takes a variety of forms, and so you need to think specifically about what you can do with *your* data, with *your* learners, in *your* classroom. This seems obvious, but sometimes those concerned with huge datasets can be distanced from the learners, and be solely concerned with numbers on a spreadsheet. You, on the other hand, will know your learners, and, importantly, know their names, how well they are doing, their likes and dislikes, and how well (or not!) they are getting on with their learning. It's how to put all this together that we will be looking at today.

Today's strategies

* Assessment and learning:

    1. Formative use of summative assessment

    2. Assessment as learning (not a bolt-on)

* Using assessment data:

    3. Target setting

    4. Using assessment data to plan for learning

* Thinking about learning

    5. How have I done?

    6. Not starting from scratch

Strategy: Assessment and learning

When thinking about assessment and learning, sometimes assessment is regarded as following on from learning. Today the aim is to change that to assessment preceding learning, going from this:

to this, where assessment data is used to inform teaching:

Notice too that in this second version assessment and teaching interact with each other. It is not simply a one-way stream of information!

1. Formative use of summative assessment

This may seem like a mouthful, but it is how schools often use summative assessment data. In fact, in some places the formative use of summative assessment is sometimes mistaken for proper formative assessment. In the formative use of summative assessment, grades, marks, and so on are used to determine not only how well a learner is doing, but also what to do next. This can be really helpful in deciding what to do, for instance, if a learner has been scoring badly, and some sort of intervention is necessary. Similarly, it can indicate who needs stretching to achieve even more. Knowing this from summative assessment data gives you the chance to do something about it formatively!

2. Assessment as learning (not a bolt-on)

We know that the purposeful application of summative assessment in the form of regular testing can actually increase learning. This is because testing places the retrieval of things that have already been learned to the fore, and actually improves retention of what has been learned already. It is probably better for the classroom if this takes the form of fairly frequent low-stakes quizzes, such as those introduced on Day 3, rather than high-stakes exams.

What this means is that assessment becomes a part of the teaching and learning processes themselves, rather than being just a 'bolt-on' as in the first diagram in this chapter. Thinking of assessment as learning in this way is an important reconceptualisation for teachers and schools, which sometimes talk about assessment as though it is separated and isolated from learning.

Ms Stakes is a Year 6 class teacher in a primary school. Her class will be doing SATs later, so she is keen for them to do as well as they can. To this end she employs daily quizzes on what has been learned the previous day. She makes these low stakes, and as much fun as she can, mixing quick-fire recall questions which she reads out with slightly longer written questions which require thinking. For manageability, she gets the learners themselves to mark each other's work, the quick-fire ones being essentially right-or-wrong answers, whereas for longer answers she has a list of key words which learners need to have included to score. Again, she gets learners to mark their own work according to key words. At the end of the week, the table with the highest scores, or most improvement, or best answers, or neatest work, gets some sort of reward. She varies these, so it is not always the same high-scoring learners who are rewarded.

A Spot of Theory

Dunlosky et al found that practice tests were a highly effective way of improving learning:

Testing effects have been demonstrated across an impressive range of practice-test formats, kinds of material, learner ages, outcome measures, and retention intervals. Thus, practice testing has broad applicability. Practice testing is not particularly time-intensive relative to other techniques, and it can be implemented with minimal training.

(Dunlosky et al, 2013, p 35)

Asking quick fire questions

Strategy: Using assessment data

In schools, there are a number of common ways you will find assessment data being put to use centrally, which will in turn affect your own teaching and learning. Your own assessment data, as you have seen, will also have an important part to play though, as the next two strategies demonstrate.

3. Target setting

In many schools and colleges you will be set targets for your learners to achieve, derived from statistical software packages. These are useful, but it is also important to be able to use your own assessment data in all its rich variety for setting individual and personalised targets for your learners. This can be done using a mixture of formative and summative assessment data. Formative data is really important in helping you know your learners, and what steps they need to take next. Allied with summative data from tests and quizzes, this can be a powerful tool in formulating individual learning targets.

All too often, targets can be variations of the 'do better next time' variety. Using your knowledge of the learners:

- think about how you could help a learner *specifically* improve on something they find difficult;

- provide an achievable, small step for a learner to succeed at to build up their self-confidence;

- provide a targeted behaviour-related outcome for a learner to help them in class;

- suggest a way that a learner could try something different;

- provide a short list of facts that a learner can use for a forthcoming quiz, in an area in which they usually struggle.

4. Using assessment data to plan for learning

You can use assessment data to plan for learning in very specific ways, too. Once again, a combination of formative data from conversations you have had with the learners and summative data from tests and quizzes will help inform your decisions on the specifics of what to teach *next*, and what topics or subjects would benefit from being revisited. This does not alter the overall direction of learning, but instead focuses in on these learners, in this class, in this specific lesson.

This sort of planning for learning is very much of the reactive sort. It cannot be done much in advance, but depends on your own assessment data – not the statistical packages mentioned earlier – being used essentially to tweak existing plans. This really focuses your attention onto the wants and needs of *your* learners in the moment, as you are working with the real class you have in front of you.

Miss Kaur teaches secondary-school mathematics. She regularly gives her Key Stage 3 learners quick-fire quizzes. She has noticed that one class in particular are not doing as well as she would have hoped in calculating complex areas. She has talked to the learners, and knows that one of the issues that keeps coming up is the comment *'I can't do maths'*. She decides to produce a series of five targets for her learners, based on her knowledge of what they are not able to do:

1. To do 10 multiplication calculations correctly;
2. To measure the sides of a shape accurately;
3. To know how to calculate the area of a simple shape;
4. To know how to calculate the area of a triangle;
5. To know how to estimate the area of an irregular shape by simplification.

She then distributes these on small printouts individually to learners she has decided they are appropriate for, with the aim that they will each have achieved them by the end of the week.

★ What might this look like in your own teaching context?

★ How do you know what the targets should be?

★ How can you work out which are the common issues?

★ How can you ensure your targets are specific and relevant?

All of these can be answered by the careful use of evidence from assessment data.

A Spot of Theory

According to Black and Wiliam:

...pupils can assess themselves only when they have a sufficiently clear picture of the targets that their learning is meant to attain. Surprisingly, and sadly, many pupils do not have such a picture, and they appear to have become accustomed to receiving classroom teaching as an arbitrary sequence of exercises with no overarching rationale.

(Black and Wiliam, 1998, p 142)

Strategy: Thinking about learning

It may seem obvious to say that the point of teaching is to promote learning, but sometimes being in the classroom is such a busy activity that we end up thinking more about teaching than we do about learning! The strategies that we are considering here involve thinking about using assessment data to help with learning that results from your teaching.

5. How have I done?

Learners will ask you, *'How have I done?'* at every possible opportunity. But you will also want to ask yourself this question too! So, how can you use assessment data to investigate what learning has resulted from your teaching? Here are some things to think about.

- Ask individual learners direct questions about what they are doing.
- What does this questioning reveal about misconceptions they may have?
- They haven't scored as well as you thought on the last quiz. Why?
- Use test scores to grade your own teaching of a topic. What mark do you get? Should your mark be an average of their scores?
- What's the hardest question on this topic you could ask them? Can they answer it?
- What's a very easy answer on this topic, and can they all answer that?

6. Not starting from scratch

Whenever learners move from one context to another there can be a danger that teachers assume that the learners don't know anything about their subject, and so they start again from scratch. Primary school teachers tend to get very aggrieved when secondary schools do this, as do secondary schools with further education colleges! Wiliam and Black observe that:

> *one way of asking a question might produce no answer from the student, while a slightly different approach may elicit evidence of achievement. We can never be absolutely sure that we have exhausted all the possibilities, so that we can never be sure that the student does not know something, but some assessments will be better than others in this respect.*

> *(Wiliam and Black, 1996, p 541)*

Are you always definitely sure your learners do not know something? Here are some other questions to consider:

- How could you find out what the learners have already covered?
- How can you try to find out what they don't know?
- Is declarative knowledge (being able to speak/write about a topic) sufficient?
- What about knowing how to do something in your subject area?
- What if learners don't know what they have previously covered?
- Does your school or college have a link tutor who visits at key transition points?

Choose a topic that you have been teaching recently. Then think about these issues:

Choose five learners at random (really at random!).

* How well do they know the topic?

* In what order of attainment would you put these learners?

* Which learner would you be confident could explain to a colleague what they had been learning?

* Which learner would you not want to do this!?

* If your teaching were to be judged on the basis of these five learners, how well would you come out?

Some observations:

* What assessment data do you have as evidence of formative assessment?

* How does your formative assessment link with your summative assessment data?

* Is it possible to find out if your formative comments have been acted upon in the course of a busy lesson?

* Have you spoken to everyone in your class? How do you know?

* What question would you not want a colleague to ask this class about your teaching of this topic?

A Spot of Theory

The major message is for teachers to pay attention to the formative effects of their teaching, as it is these attributes of seeking evaluation of the effects (intended or unintended) of their programs that makes for excellence in teaching.

(Hattie, 2009, p 24)

Checklist

Use this to keep a record of what worked well for you and what didn't. A strategy that works with one class may not work so well with another. Keeping a checklist helps you to work out what factors or learner characteristics call for one approach rather than another. There's a line at the bottom for you to add your own most frequently used strategy, if it's not already included in the list.

Strategy	Tried it with...	On...(date)	It worked	It didn't work	Worth trying again?
1. **Formative use of summative assessment***					
2. Assessment as learning (not a bolt-on)					
3. Target setting					
4. Using assessment data to plan for learning					
5. How have I done?					
6. Not starting from scratch					
Your own strategy?					

DAY 6: You need some grades – now!

You have seen throughout this book that there are all sorts of ways and means by which you can integrate assessment into the teaching and learning which takes place in your classroom. Today's activities focus on those times when you will assess to produce grades. This may seem an odd thing to say. Surely, you say, teachers are producing grades all the time? But some subjects are more grade-generative than others! But, whatever it is that you are doing, whether producing grades as a matter of course, or because the deputy head said they need them by half past three on Friday, let's think about what this entails.

Today's strategies

* What are you doing?
  1. Data and its uses (and abuses)
* How do you record it?
  2. Mark books
* What is evidence?
  3. What counts as work?
  4. Process and product
* How else can you do it?
  5. Comparative assessment
* Moderate with / phone a friend!
  6. Moderation
* Exam preparation
  7. Preparing for statutory testing

Strategy: What are you doing?

Day 4 looked at assessment data, and who the audiences for this might be. The chapter discussed how this data could be used for tracking, and other purposes. In this strategy, you need to think very carefully about the assessment data you generate. Here are some questions to ask yourself.

- ✹ Does everything you give a grade to carry the same weight?
- ✹ Are all marks given in something you grade, equal?
- ✹ Are there different ways by which learners could arrive at a mark of, say 7/10?
- ✹ When you give a total mark, is its meaning transparent?
- ✹ How reliable is your grading? If you have a bad headache, or are in a bad mood, will this affect your grading?
- ✹ Are your colleagues identical in their marking? Are some more generous than others?
- ✹ Do you mark details, or do you go for 'big picture' marking?
- ✹ Do *marking* and *grading* mean the same thing?

In thinking about these questions, it should become clear that not all data is created equal! Indeed, there is a whole industry looking at whether a qualification in hairdressing is equal to one in motor mechanics, or nuclear physics.

1. Data and its uses (and abuses)

What we want you to think about is the question, *'How good is my data?'*. And for this we ask a similar question to one asked before, *'What is the purpose of the assessment data?'*. If your salary depends on how well your learners do in tests, then you will want them to do jolly well indeed, and will put a lot of effort into this. If it is simply a semi-informal quiz, that only you will know the answer to, then maybe less effort on your part will go into preparing the learners for this.

Miss Queue-Tee has been told by her assistant-headteacher that she wants her grades by home time on Thursday. Miss Queue-Tee teaches art, and has only been in the school for a month, and it is her NQT year. She has seen the Key Stage 3 classes twice in that time, as they are on a fortnightly timetable. Her NQT colleagues in mathematics, by comparison, have seen their classes 20 times already over this same timeframe. What can she do? She is worried! Here are some suggestions.

A.   Ask the learners to undertake a very simple drawing task, which they will then be graded as having completed using a three-point scale:

★   Can nearly do this;

★   Can do this;

★   Can do this well.

Miss Queue-Tee can then simply convert the statements, which she can assess very rapidly, into a three-point scale, grading 1, for 'can nearly do this', 2 for 'can do this', and 3 for 'can do this well' (see Fautley and Daubney (2015) for a worked example of this three-part grading system). This will very rapidly give her a set of grades she can build on, as these can also be a baseline assessment.

B.   Be honest, and say, 'I have only taught them twice, I have been concentrating on seeing what they can do, and I am making a baseline assessment based on what they can do'. We must remember that sometimes SLTs 'forget'(!) that some subjects are not taught as frequently as others, and need reminding!

C.   Miss Queue-Tee is an art teacher; she can go with a digital portfolio of exemplar work, and say, 'This is what they have done so far. I will be grading their work at the end of this project, in three lessons' time (that's six weeks, for the mathematics teachers!). This is all work in progress'.

D.   Ask her head of department what she does, and take her advice. She offers to look at the work done so far together, and they jointly grade according to the school assessment policy.

★   What would this look like for you, in your teaching context?

A Spot of Theory

Adrian Mole said: 'Got full marks in the geography test today. Yes, I am proud to report that I got twenty out of twenty! ... There is nothing I don't know about the Norwegian leather industry'

(Townsend, 1983, p 72–73).

★   Does Adrian Mole's assessment data really mean that?

Strategy: How do you record it?

You have seen that assessments create marks and grades; the issue for you as a teacher is: what do you do with them?

2. Mark books

Mark books have come a long way from simply being handwritten collections of squared paper. But for some teachers, this old-school method is the one they prefer. Well, fair enough! But we also have all sorts of high-tech digital ways of storing grades, and these can do a lot more than simply store a number. They also have the advantage that so long as you have saved them properly, you are less likely to lose them!

- Does your school or college have a storage system you have to use?
- What is it?
- What does it entail?
- How do you enter marks into it?

Knowing what your school, college or academy does is a vital first stage in working out how you will be collecting and storing grades. Importantly, it will also affect your *thinking* about grades. ICT systems that only permit grades to be entered as, say, marks out of 10, will mean you have to think differently about how you grade from ones which are more free-form in nature.

But, if your context has a digital system, what else can it do? In the example above, an art teacher wanted to show her learners' artwork. Some e-platforms allow the uploading of images; does yours? This can also help with examples of learners' written work. What about audio or video for PE, drama, and music teachers? What else can image-uploading do? Building up an evidence portfolio of work over time is far more meaningful for you, the learners, and their parents than simply a collection of numbers. Can your e-platform do this, and do you know how to exploit it to your learners' advantage?

Miss Queue-Tee, our secondary school art teacher, has found that her school has a digital assessment management system that allows her to enter grades in subdivided numbers 1c–9a format, but also to enter comments as free text and images. She decides that she will upload photos of her learners' work to this e-system each time they complete something. She sets about keeping a careful record of her learners' work.

One thing that she notices very early on is that with lots of learners to work with, she has to be very careful with naming files. Simply allowing each one to be called some random computer-generated number isn't helpful. She goes in search of the ICT department, who tell her about file naming conventions, and how she can do this. She decides to name each image with the learner's name and the date, so she can look back and see how progression has taken place. The ICT people help her with this, and she now has the beginnings of her record system, which she will add to over time.

A Spot of Theory

When assessment is focused on the classroom, the professional status of teachers is enhanced … the use of performance assessment type tasks serves as a powerful professional development tool when teachers are involved in the design and marking of such tasks. In addition, teachers' involvement in assessment moderation and standard setting are invaluable in helping them to assign performance levels correctly according to national standards.

(Stanley et al, 2009, p 6)

Strategy: What is evidence?

You have been thinking about assessment data, but, like our art teacher, maybe you too are wondering what actually counts as assessment data, and what is the evidence that you might need to support it?

3. What counts as work?

This might seem another odd question! But what counts as work depends on your teaching context. Maybe in your context it is very obvious – it's what's in your learners' books. But what if you teach PE? Material in books might be very slight if you have been teaching rugby, possibly? So what counts as work depends on what you have been teaching, what this looks like, and how it manifests itself.

4. Process and product

A key instance of what counts as work for assessment purposes is with regard to *process* and *product*. Some learning results in an end product, an artefact, an outcome or end result. But in order to get to this end product, the learner needs to go through a series of stages in order to reach it. The famous example is in mathematics, where learners are instructed to 'show your working'. We think it normal to award marks for the stages of a complex calculation, even if the final answer is wrong. Likewise, in science we accept that grades can be awarded even if the outcome wasn't as expected.

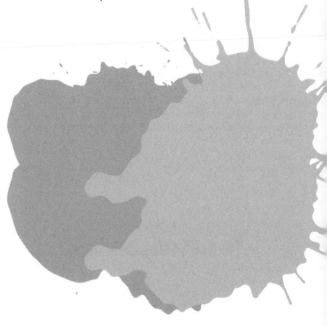

- So, what does this look like in your teaching?
- Where do you award marks for process, and where for product?
- How important is it that the final product is perfect?
- How much do you want to know about the learning and working en route to the final product?

Process marking

Miss Milton is teaching poetry to her Year 7 English class. She has been working on syllabic structure with them, and they have been writing limericks to help them with this. The important thing Miss Milton wants them to learn to start with is the metre of the limerick, and she has given them some examples to look at, and to read out loud in class, including some she had written for them:

> *There was a young lady from Bath*
> *Who looked like a clumsy giraffe.*
> *With her very long neck*
> *And her clothes coloured check,*
> *She had trouble untying her scarf!*

She has asked the class to write the first two lines only, which she then asks them to read. The final limericks, she hopes, will be at least as good as hers, but at the moment she is *only* interested in the first two lines. Her marking scheme looks like this:

	Nowhere near! (1 mark)	Close (2 marks)	Yes! (3 marks)
Syllabic structure			
Rhyme			
Makes sense			

These will be marks for process, and for work in progress. Notice we haven't reached the final limerick stage yet.

 What would the equivalent of this be for you, in the context of your own teaching?

A Spot of Theory

In her study of assessment, Wynne Harlen (2005, p 214) recommended that 'Changing teachers' assessment practices to include processes and explanations leads to better student learning'.

Strategy: How else can you do it?

5. Comparative assessment

When you are really busy – and let's face it, this happens a lot in teaching – then other ways of marking would be helpful. Comparative assessment, also known as comparative judgement, derives from the work of Thurstone back in 1927, where he observed that, *'People are better at making relative judgements than absolute judgements'* (Ofqual, 2015, p 7). Nowadays, comparative assessment is becoming popular, and it may well be the case that your institution is involved in using it. In essence, it involves looking at two pieces of work, and deciding which is best, then looking at two more, and then keeping on looking at pairs until they all have been placed into rank order. It helps if you can have a lot of examples, and it also helps if there is more than one person making the judgements; there are websites which help with this.

This all sounds a bit wacky, as you are not poring over work with assessment criteria, but instead simply deciding which one of two pieces of work is best. Of course, it is useful if the work is in a format that allows easy comparison, but this approach can be applied in other instances too, for example drama teachers looking at videos of learners on stage.

One advantage of this system is that, in the words of Tom Bramley, *'...it does not matter how good (in absolute terms) they [the judges] think the scripts they are judging are: all that matters is their relative merit'* (Bramley, 2007, p 247).

It may well be worth you seeing if there is a comparative assessment group in your school, your Multi-Academy Trust (MAT), or your area, as over time this could save you some work!

Comparative assessment

Mr Norman is head of history in a secondary school. The school sets formal end-of-year examinations for all classes from Year 7 onwards, and so Mr Norman and his team have a lot of marking to do at exam time. This year, for a change, Mr Norman decides that the team of three history teachers will all do a comparative judgement exercise using the Year 9 examination, where the learners have been set an essay under examination conditions.

Mr Norman and his colleagues each begin by reading two of the scripts from one of the Year 9 classes. They then decide which of the two is best. They then choose another script, and do the same, but with of the ones of they have just decided upon. They continue this process of comparing a new script with the ones they have already decided upon until they have done all the scripts in that class. Mr Norman then decides that at that point they will compare the scripts from another class using the same technique.

After a while they get much quicker at this. At no stage so far during this process have any of the teachers written anything down about the scripts. The processes continues until they have rank ordered the scripts. The final few take far less time than the first ones.

From this the teachers decide they can identify, and subsequently write, generic statements of qualitative response which they can employ both to the learners, and for reporting. This they do, and although initially the process was slow, over time they got much quicker.

A Spot of Theory

Alastair Pollitt says this about comparative judgement:

Professional judgement by teachers replaces the marking of tests; a judge is asked to compare the work of two students and simply to decide which of them is the better. From many such comparisons a measurement scale is created showing the relative quality of students' work; this can then be referenced in familiar ways to generate test results.

(Pollitt, 2012, p 281)

Strategy: Moderate with / phone a friend!

You are not alone! You will have friends, maybe that you trained with, or in your department, or in another school. Moderation, the process of scrutinising learner work to see if the grades awarded are fair and reasonable, can be a daunting thing to begin with. But if a few of you can get together, this can really help. We saw with comparative assessment how this can be done, and the same approach can be applied to moderation.

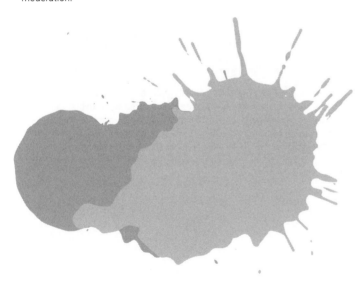

6. Moderation

Once you have marked and graded some work, and before assessment data gets entered into the school system, some schools expect some form of moderation process to have taken place. For smaller subjects, and in smaller schools, this can be a real issue. But equip yourself with coffee, wine, or whatever, invite a few friendly colleagues from other schools or colleges round one evening, and ask them to bring a sample of learners' work with them. It helps if they can bring around a few from the top, middle and lower marks awarded, and then you discuss what you think about the work. Importantly, this also helps you gain a view as to the different standards operating in and between schools.

You can also do this within a single school, and this gives all the staff an overview as to what is happening in other teachers' classrooms, and with their assessments.

Either way, this is a helpful way of getting to know about assessment and standards. Too often, new and inexperienced teachers can be left alone. Moderating with a friend helps dispel anxiety and might also give you some new curriculum ideas to develop in your own teaching!

In St Joseph's Primary School, there is a long-established moderation process for looking at learners' work. St Joseph's is a two-form entry primary school, and at the end of each half-term the teachers get together and pair up in year groups, so there are four teachers talking together. This has become quite a social occasion too, and there is a prize for the best home-cooked cake! The teachers bring with them a range of work from different learners in their classes, and talk about the marks and grades they have given. The headteacher circulates, and has a look in on all of the discussions at some point.

Apart from enjoying the cake, what the teachers at St Joseph's have found is that talking with their colleagues helps them really get a feel for how their classes are doing. It also helps with inter-year work, as the teachers from different parts of the school can see first hand what work has been done by the learners.

At the end of the moderation session, some grades are altered, and these are then used as a sort of 'barometer' as to how the rest of the class fit in to the range of work that has been seen.

A Spot of Theory

Writing about the moderation process, Paul Black and colleagues note:

Moderation across schools was generally successful and the project teachers were, in most cases, able to agree on a national curriculum level *[not that we have these any more, of course!]* for each of the portfolios that they examined. These samples, with the agreed levels, could then be used as reference standards for all. However, what was also important was the learning of the teachers as they established communal standards through grappling with differences between their own judgements and those of their colleagues. In a minority of cases, these differences could be quite large.

(Black et al, 2010, p 225)

Strategy: Exam preparation

7. Preparing for statutory testing

Whatever it is that you have been teaching, there comes a point for many teachers where you have to prepare to enter your learners for examinations set by external agencies. Of course, for many teachers this is the whole raison d'être of their teaching, in that the learners have been aiming for external testing from the outset. Whatever the case may be, there are some important things you can do to check that your learners are ready for the big day!

One of the key things you can do is to prepare your learners for the conditions of the examination itself, in terms of what they will be expected to do. Past papers are ideal for this, but a past paper alone is not sufficient. You will need to explain *how* to answer specific types of questions. This will be relevant and specific to your context, but it is important that you do not just give learners past papers, but that you spend some time dissecting with them what it is that they will need to do in a specific question type. What this means for you is that you need to know what the examiners are looking for in the questions that they are setting. You need to either get hold of a past mark-scheme, if it exists, or really think about what the question is asking, and what the candidates need to do to maximise their potential grading from it.

While it can seem like trial exams and past papers take away from learning time, it is important to think not only about what has been learned, but what a specific question is asking for. This is as true for SATs as for A levels. Taking time to prepare learners so that they know about different question types is as important as actually ensuring that the topics have been covered in the first place.

What are the hidden attributes?

Beware of 'trap' questions

Preparing for exams

Mrs Biggs is head of geography in a secondary school. Her team are preparing learners for examination entry at GCSE level. Mrs Biggs has set a specific date by which point all of the syllabus needs to have been covered, so that the rest of the time can be spent on exam and question preparation, not on covering new material. The geography team have been very carefully analysing past papers, and have divided up the job between them so they each concentrate on specific areas. They have also written some new questions, following the format of the previous ones, in areas that are appropriate to the programme of study. They then rotate the teaching between the three groups that they will be entering for the examination, with each teacher dealing with the specific areas of focus for which they have responsibility. They also mark and grade the answers the learners provide, and offer feedback for improvement.

Activity

Look at some past papers for your subject area or context. Do the following:

* Make a list of question types asked. Ignore the content, just look at the type of question being asked.

* What specific phraseology is being employed in questions? Is there a specific meaning that questions of this type are intended to investigate?

* Try to work out what the mark distribution for a particular question is. Many examinations print the available marks by the question. If you have a mark-scheme, this should help.

* What are the *hidden* attributes that the examination is investigating? What does it seem to want the learners to know that it is not asking directly?

* What are the 'trap' questions that the learners could fall into? Is there a commonality to these?

Having done this, think about the ways in which *you* can prepare *your* learners to answer these types of questions. What do you need to do? How do you need to do it? What do they need to know and understand in order to do well?

Remember, good examination preparation is not just about having covered the content; it is also about preparing the learners to maximise their potential to demonstrate this.

A Spot of Theory

Daniel Koretz distinguishes between seven different types of test preparation:

* *working more effectively;*
* *teaching more;*
* *working harder;*
* *reallocation;*
* *alignment;*
* *coaching;*
* *cheating.*

He notes that the first three types are what proponents of high-stakes testing want to see.

(Koretz, 2009, p 251)

Checklist

Use this to keep a record
of what worked well for
you and what didn't.
A strategy that works with
one class may not work so
well with another. Keeping
a checklist helps you to
work out what factors or
learner characteristics call
for one approach rather
than another. There's a
line at the bottom for you
to add your own most
frequently used strategy, if
it's not already included in
the list.

Strategy	Tried it with...	On...(date)	It worked	It didn't work	Worth trying again?
1. Data and its uses (and abuses)					
2. Mark books					
3. What counts as work?					
4. Process and product*					
5. Comparative assessment					
6. Moderate with / phone a friend!					
7. Preparing for statutory testing					
Your own strategy?					

DAY 7: Master of the assessment universe!

Having worked your way through this book, you should now have a reasonable understanding of the many and versatile uses for assessment, as well as a whole raft of practical strategies to try out in your own teaching. As Eisner (1996, p 4) reminds us:

> It is important to recognize at the outset that assessment in education has various functions, each distinctive and requiring distinctive tactics and methods… Once diverse assessment functions are identified, the press towards a universal one-size-fits-all approach to assessment diminishes, a more complex view of assessment emerges, and the options one can consider expand.

This chapter moves towards longer-term ways in which meaningful and ethical assessment practices can be developed, and suggests how sharing learners' own work and ideas provides a platform for further development. It also encourages you to consider the uniqueness of each subject or learning area and explore ways to collect, use and celebrate work over time. The chapter also provides a framework for you to reflect on the development of your knowledge and experiences of a range of assessment ideas and then to consider how your understanding of the relationship between curriculum, pedagogy and assessment may have developed.

Today's strategies

1. Exemplar work – finding examples of learners' work, and modelling marking and feedback on this

2. Peer marking – developing the above in relation to their own and each other's work

3. Portfolios – try this! Showing a learning journey

4. Find and improve best work – looking back over what has been done and asking, 'Where is there good work?' and 'How does this show progress over time?'

5. Personal constructs – designing personal constructs (PCs) relating to a theme, and setting targets from them

6. How do you know they know, or don't? – deciding whether, now you know all of this, you would define learning differently

7. Celebrating work – trying different ways to do this throughout the year, rather than just at report time

Strategy: Exemplar work – finding examples of learners' work, and modelling marking and feedback on this

Introduction

Using examples of work can be a very effective way for learners to engage with materials in different ways and to understand and recognise what is good about something, what could be improved and how this might happen. In order to ensure that learners do not think they are seeking the one 'right' answer, it can be useful to share a range of exemplar work. Using exemplar marking during the process of learning, rather than at the end, has the potential to provide new ideas and approaches for learners to try out in their own work. Exemplar work can also help learners to better understand marking or success criteria and reflect on their own work in relation to the criteria. It also means that you can model the marking process so that it is transparent.

Marking anonymised exemplar work can also help learners be more objective about the work they are marking, since it allows them to put aside any personal feelings about the work and the learners who may have produced it.

1. Exemplar work

All work that learners undertake has some 'hallmarks' of success, whether or not these are tightly defined. In this strategy, learners are given exemplar work in an accessible form – for example, a written example video, soundtrack or physical example of something. They may be given work at different levels. Assuming that learners already have an understanding of what 'success' will look/sound like in this particular context, they will use

the exemplar work to think about the relative strengths, weaknesses and areas for development. You may want to think about providing a framework for this through some questions, such as:

- What are the strengths of this work? What works really well? What do you like? Is there anything that surprised you or that you might not have thought about?

- How do the strengths relate to the success criteria? How will you explain to the person who produced the work how their work is reflected in the things identified that make this successful?

- What have you spotted that could be improved or developed?

- If you were to give feedback, what would you suggest as 'next steps' to improve this work further?

- (If appropriate in this specific situation.) What mark would you allocate the work and why?

The class are writing their own war poetry. They have studied famous poems and discussed the context of the poems, generating a list together of things that make war poetry successful. These include the communication of mood, feelings and context, as well as conventions such as starting new lines with a capital letter.

Year 8 English teacher Mrs Owen distributes a range of anonymised poems labelled A, B, C, D, E, F and G, which were produced by the year above in the previous academic year. She shows the criteria on the board and asks learners to look through their poem in pairs and work their way through the questions above. As they do this she moves from group to group, listening in to the emergent conversations, chipping in with comments, suggestions or questions as necessary. After five minutes she instructs learners to find the pair in the room with the same poem as them and discuss what they have decided about the quality of the work.

Reflective questions – exemplar work

- How could you emulate Mrs Owen's approach in your own context?

- Do learners have the necessary subject-specific vocabulary to be able to talk about work in this way? Might this provide a learning opportunity for them?

- If you trial doing this, see if it helps your learners understand what it is you are looking for when you undertake marking and grading of their work. Does it?

- Do you have examples of good work from previous learners that you could use for this purpose?

- If you are new to your school or college, do your colleagues keep examples which may be useful for this purpose?

- How do you convey to the learners what a good example of what you are looking for in an assessment task entails?

- If you work in a team, do you know if you and your colleagues share the same understandings of what quality work entails? Might sharing examples of work done by learners maybe hep with this?

- Doing this over time means that you will build up a considerable bank of resources. Ask your IT people about what systems they can suggest that would help with storage and retrieval of this work. Does your context have these in place already?

A Spot of Theory

A systematic review of what children aged 11–16 believe impacts on their motivation to learn reports that:

The way that assessment of the curriculum is constructed and practised in school appears to influence how pupils see themselves as learners and social beings.

(Smith et al, 2005, p 4)

Strategy: Peer marking – developing the above in relation to their own and each other's work

Introduction

At the most basic level, peer marking can mean simply swapping papers and marking each other's work on a right/wrong basis. Yet there is so much more potentially to gain from peer marking.

Once you have established a framework for exemplar marking based upon anonymised exemplar material, it is more straightforward to get learners to give peer feedback and mark each other's work. It is possible to do peer marking without having established an objective and thoughtful way of marking exemplar work first, but you will need to spend some time developing a supportive culture and making sure that objectivity is central.

There are many opportunities for giving peer feedback during a learning process. Peer marking does not necessarily need to happen at the end – it could also happen during the process and provide formative guidance from which the work can be further developed.

2. Peer marking

As with marking exemplar work, this strategy works well if there is a clear framework of expectation about how to provide developmental feedback in a positive and supportive way, and there is a common understanding of the hallmarks of 'success'. Note that this does not need to be in the form of a shopping list – it can be more broadly defined. Indeed, defining 'success criteria' as a shopping list can stifle creativity and exploration. You could work through a series of questions, as in the previous example, and these could be in a written or verbal format. What is important is that learners who are marking are able to justify the marks and comments given, and that the way in which these are communicated is clear, understandable and forward-looking.

A Spot of Theory

Peer assessment is part of our daily lives – learners already do this in a variety of different ways. Race (2001) defines many advantages of involving learners in peer marking, including helping them understand the culture of assessment, helping learners to achieve deep learning and learning from the approaches, successes and mistakes of others.

The Year 7 art class have been making their own stop motion animations using cardboard, modelling clay, wire and mixed media. Having filmed their animations, the groups are paired up to watch each other's videos and mark them in relation to the criteria developed together in the first lesson of this unit. A very simple mark scheme has been drawn up for learners to complete and then provide feedback to the work's creators.

Following this, the class were given more time to develop their work, starting with some planning time to decide on what they would do next and how they would do this. The peer marking was used as a basis for generating the 'what next' ideas.

Criteria	Fully	Partly	Not yet	Suggestions for future improvement
Storyline makes sense and is in a logical order				
Characters communicate with each other				
Is visually engaging (scenery)				
Music/sound/silence is effective and contributes to the mood				

If you were the film critic, what can you identify that is excellent in the film so far?

●

●

●

If the animators only had time to work on improving one aspect, what do you think they should focus on?

●

Strategy: Portfolios – try this! Showing a learning journey

Introduction

In a classroom situation, work is produced over a very long period of time and making a portfolio is a fantastic way of capturing the work, celebrating the work and having something that really shows changes and developments over time. An effective portfolio is owned by the learners – something which they can be proud of and want to share with others. Across early years settings, the creation of portfolios is part of everyday practice. Portfolios can be mixed media – including, for example, audio, physical examples of work, photographs, commentaries and comments. In art, the creation of a portfolio in the form of a sketchbook is commonplace; this is fantastic as it values the process as much as the resultant product. There is untapped potential in education for the process to be valued and valuable; indeed, it is often overlooked. The question is, what would a portfolio look/sound like if it was more widely used? There are many ways to create portfolios and many tools to help.

3. Portfolios

The portfolio might just be from one subject or learning area, or potentially relate to learning in (and possibly out of) school. We need to think about the purpose of the portfolio and whom it is for. Depending upon the answers to this, we can work out how the portfolio is collected, shared and its potential role in assessment.

Over the course of the year/project/term, encourage learners to document part of the learning process. Hopefully they are doing this anyway in order to take a reflective approach to learning. Find a meaningful way to collect and collate this – it might be through a scrapbook, a blog or an online learning environment. It can be brought to life through visual examples and further enhanced through audio and video. For example, learners may record themselves talking about their work and reflecting upon it. In curriculum areas such as drama, dance and music it makes sense to use video to capture work.

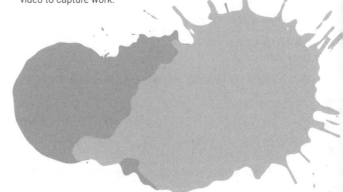

In music, if you do not capture sound in real time, you often have nothing left, and so making regular audio (or video) recording part of your armoury is vitally important and is arguably the most useful way for learners to engage in their own music and reflect upon it. You could use an audio portfolio as a 'sound scrapbook' of ideas or works in progress, and play this back, thus encouraging learners to listen to their own work in order to improve it further and then to share it. In this example, the lower secondary school class works mostly in groups and have an online free cloud-based digital portfolio where their work throughout the year can be uploaded and discussed. There is one page for the whole class.

Towards the end of a lesson, a group of Year 8 learners performed a work-in-progress version of a folk song they have been composing, which was audio-recorded on the teacher's mobile phone. The group and the teacher discussed the merits of the work, the intent and compositional and creative ideas, what they wanted to achieve next, and how they might go about this. The conversation was also recorded. The recording of the performance and discussion were uploaded, as part of the class portfolio, to the class's page on the online environment. At the beginning of the following lesson, the group listened back to their work and the discussion and had a few minutes planning time before continuing with developing their folk song.

A Spot of Theory

Portfolios have long been recognised as a powerful tool in early years education. Recent qualifications for practical or work-related subjects (for example BTEC, PE and music) exploit the use of these to capture process. Their general use across education has also developed over recent years (eg Kember, nd).

Strategy: Find and improve best work – looking back over what has been done and asking, 'Where is there good work?' and 'How does this show progress over time?'

Introduction

If, as the previous strategy suggests, learners build some kind of portfolio of work, then it is possible and desirable to be able to use this to identify and share progress over time. As learning continues, there is great potential to go back and revisit previous work, developing it in new directions or with fresh ideas now that learners are more experienced. In some areas of life, this attitude that something is 'never finished' is totally accepted. For example, branding logos are refreshed; designs of football shirts are updated. There is definitely scope for this kind of thinking to be applied more in education, so that revisiting work many weeks or months later becomes commonplace as part of the learning process.

4. Find and improve best work

If learners have a catalogue of work over time, in whatever format, it can be inspiring to look and/or listen back to, so as to identify and celebrate the work itself and to recognise the progress it demonstrates over time. This progress may not jump out as being instantly measurable but might, for example, indicate a growing sophistication of thoughts and ideas. If reflection points are added into the structure of the school year, for example in the final half term, this creates a useful framework for learners to spend some time going back through their work, revisiting the ideas, identifying favourite bits of work or ways of working and choosing some examples to rework or use as a stimulus to develop further, related work.

At the end of the academic year, the Year 4 class mount an exhibition of their favourite work to share with their teachers, family and friends. In order to prepare for this, the class spend two afternoons looking at and listening to their own work from throughout the year, which has been collected in their books and through a digital portfolio. Some of the work is individual, while some has been done in groups and some as a whole class. Each learner is tasked with identifying two pieces of written work – one they are most proud of and one they can see could be brilliant if they went to it with fresh ideas and spent some time revising it. They also choose two pieces of artwork each to display and two pieces of music they have developed as a class. Over the final two weeks before the exhibition, learners work to develop the pieces they have identified and create ways to show that they recognised their progress over time. This is achieved by each writing a reflective blog of their journey through Year 4, which signposts different pieces of work.

Reflective questions

- There are many ways that the work done by your learners will develop over time. Two obvious examples are *breadth* and *depth*. How could you use portfolios to exemplify the ways your learners have shown such developments?

- Think about the work your learners produce. What sort of portfolio would suit this best? Paper? Electronic? Video? How might this be stored, displayed, shared with parents, or accessed?

- Think about the learning journey that your learners have been on. How can they evidence that they know more, can do more, and have deeper understanding at the end than at the beginning in ways which the learners themselves will recognise?

- The internet is awash with social media. Could your learners use a social media type approach to evidence progression? What would blog posts look like over time showing progression. Would this be a suitable way for your learners?

- Some teachers and schools are rightly wary of social media. Could some form of learning diary fulfil a similar role, without recourse to the internet?

- How is learner progression assessed in your context?

- How does their attainment over time build up into a picture of progression for your learners?

A Spot of Theory

This strategy is also a way of helping learners – and teachers – to overcome 'perfectionist tendencies' by helping them to understand that the notion that something should be 'perfect' is unrealistic.

(Stoeber and Otto, 2006)

Strategy: Personal constructs – designing personal constructs (PCs) relating to a theme, and setting targets from them

Introduction

Often in assessment, we – that is, the teachers and the 'system' – decide what we want to measure and how we are going to go about it. Yet there is great value in obtaining an 'insider' viewpoint – helping you to understand how your learners see the world. Kelly (1955) came up with the theory that an individual's world is personally constructed and therefore one person's construction of the world may not be the same as another person's. Butler and Hardy's (1992) Performance Profile was developed in sport psychology as a tool to give practical application to this theory. The strategy described here uses this tool to provide an effective framework for learners to think about and share their construction of the world. The Performance Profile is also a very useful tool for setting targets and goals and a way into dialogic discussions about learning.

5. Personal constructs

In a performance profiling exercise, the individual decides on and notes down their own ideas, which are not judged as right or wrong. It is context-specific. The following steps are undertaken, and the emergent ideas are mapped onto a polar graph.

A. Decide on what is being described – eg what makes a great singer? What makes a great apprentice engineer?

B. The learner should decide for themselves the positive attributes of the person they are thinking of. One attribute should be written on the outside of each segment of the polar graph. You can see an example of a polar graph in the *Strategy in action* section which follows.

C. The learner should identify the opposite attribute, for example:
* great timekeeper / always late
* integral part of a team / individualistic
* great sense of timing / can't keep a beat

On the 0–10 scale (where zero is the lowest and 10 is the highest), the learner should colour in where they rate their own performance for each attribute. This should be repeated for all identified attributes. Conversations around this help you to understand what the learner sees as important, and also how the zero to 10 ratings develop from one rating to the next. *('You've put 6/10. Can you explain why you are a 6? What would a 7 be like?')*

D. This is an optional step, its relevance depending upon the age and experience of the learner. For more experienced/older learners you may ask them to think about how important each of these attributes is in relation to the person they are thinking of and then put them into rank order. You may also ask them to identify how good they think they should be and mark it with a line.

E. From this, learners should be encouraged to set three targets, thinking about what they want to improve and the practical steps they will take to do this.

The Year 5 music class are working on developing singing. After a session working on learning new repertoire and developing simple part-singing, Year 5 were given an eight-segment polar graph and taken through the steps above. The teacher supported some learners with the writing and after coming up with the first attribute, they were encouraged to share this with the class so that many ideas were generated. They then completed all eight segments on the polar graph, graded themselves and set targets. This was revisited in the following term. An example of the polar graph is shown below.

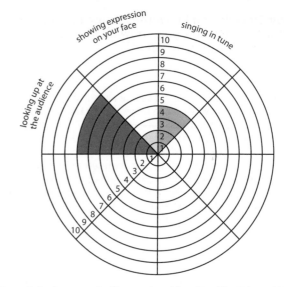

Example Performance Profile reproduced from Teaching Primary Music (Daubney, 2017, p 132)

A Spot of Theory

Research by Wanlin et al (1997) shows that people are more likely to adhere to goals if they are written down. Recording the goals and revisiting/updating the written goals periodically is therefore desirable.

Strategy: How do you know they know, or don't? – deciding whether, now you know all of this, you would define learning differently

Introduction

Throughout the book we have tried to introduce you to many different strategies for working out what learners know and don't know. As before, we are not thinking here just about 'knowing facts' but instead a whole raft of ways in which learners demonstrate what they 'know' – from your observations of their work and them working; our discussions with them; listening in to their conversations; from the responses they give to questions, whether written or discussed; from the ideas they generate – indeed, it is only from a combination of all of these that we can develop our own understanding of what they know and don't know. Remember that their voice is crucial in this – data and numbers are part of the whole picture but actually do not tell us nearly enough.

6. How do you know they know, or don't?

Think of one learner that you teach regularly. Then think about what you want them to learn. Fill in the table below, considering all the ways in which you know what they know and what they don't and how you know this. Then think about other things that they know that you hadn't considered or planned for that are also related/connected, and how you know this, too.

As you become more experienced, you may think through this in your head instead of writing it down, but mentally putting yourself in the chair of learners at different points is very helpful as a reflection framework.

What I wanted *insert name* to know:

_____

_____

What learning you planned for	Evidence for what they know/ don't know and where you get this impression from
●	
●	
What else do they know that you might not have planned for?	
●	

What do you need to do next to help guide their learning even further?

_____

_____

Effectively 'putting yourself in the chair' of one learner allows you to think about what you know about their learning, and to think about whether the challenges you designed in your lesson provided effective scaffolding for them to be able to gain access to learning and whether or not they were appropriately challenged.

Mr Khan was coming to the end of a unit on factors affecting the accuracy of eyewitness testimony with his A level psychology class. He was thinking about the effectiveness of his teaching and what learners did/didn't know, in order to guide his final two lessons. He mentally placed himself in the chair of two learners, one with generally high attainment and one with average attainment across the year. Using a combination of their recent essays, their class discussions, the interview questions they had written themselves and his observations of them during a recent role play built around a video, he realised that although both had good understanding of the impact of post-event discussion, Maawura had not grasped the significance of leading questions. Nuala had much greater depth of knowledge than he had covered in class, including knowledge of ways in which the accuracy of eyewitness testimony could be improved.

From this he was able to reflect on the strengths and weaknesses of his teaching, acknowledging that the learning in the recent role play needed to be further drawn out. He then planned the final two weeks of work, ensuring that there were opportunities to revisit the generation of questions and how these related to aspects of the cognitive interview process.

A Spot of Theory

The Teacher Assessment in Primary Science (2015) pyramid lays out multiple ways in which teachers gather the evidence and make judgements about what learners know and don't know in primary science. Aspects of this structure have uses across different subject areas and age phases.

Strategy: Celebrating work – trying different ways to do this throughout the year, rather than just at report time

Introduction

Learners spend a lot of time in school! Yet what their parents and families get to see and share might well be limited to stunted conversations generated on the way home along the lines of, *'What did you learn at school today?'* Or occasional written reports with a bunch of numbers and ticks, which may or may not be easy to interpret, and an infrequent and very short meeting with each teacher. Yet, there are definitely ways for families to share the learning and be involved in ways that help them to assess their child's learning beyond knowing whether or not they reach 'age-related expectations'. Parents will have an impoverished view of their child's education if this is all that is shared with them.

7. Celebrating work

There isn't really one specific strategy for sharing work; but here are a few different suggestions. You can probably think of others specific to your own context. Examples could include sharing work in a digital or physical portfolio; sharing via the school website; holding school events where work is shared and celebrated; and for the parent/teacher meetings to be curated by the learners. Some schools now have review days where the conversation is led by the learners and work is celebrated in a multitude of ways, for example those linked to Strategy 4 earlier in this chapter where learners spend some time selecting and developing their best work.

Celebrating hard work

Kneighton Green Primary Academy holds learning review meetings twice yearly for learners in Years 5 and 6. The class teacher, family and year leader are involved in these meetings. In preparation for these meetings, learners are encouraged to review and reflect upon their work. Through a series of questions they make a three-to-four-minute video and presentation where they summarise their learning and talk about their successes and challenges. This forms the basis of the conversation, along with the work they choose to share. Targets set in the previous learning review are revisited and new targets are set.

The questions asked are:

* What are the successes you have had in each subject area since your previous review?

* What are you most proud of in your learning since your previous review?

* What are the specific things that challenge you? What do you need to do to overcome these challenges?

* Who or what has inspired you?

* How have you inspired other people?

A Spot of Theory

Creating Learning Without Limits, *an applied research project at the University of Cambridge, developed ideas of agency and ownership of the curriculum and assessment (Swann et al, 2012).*

Checklist

Use this to keep a record of what worked well for you and what didn't. A strategy that works with one class may not work so well with another. Keeping a checklist helps you to work out what factors or learner characteristics call for one approach rather than another. There's a line at the bottom for you to add your own most frequently used strategy, if it's not already included in the list.

Strategy	Tried it with...	On...(date)	It worked	It didn't work	Worth trying again?
1. Exemplar work					
2. Peer marking					
3. Portfolios					
4. Find and improve best work					
5. Personal constructs*					
6. How do you know they know, or don't?					
7. Celebrating work					
Your own strategy?					

Further reading

Anderson, L W and Krathwohl, D R (eds) (2001) *A Taxonomy for Learning, Teaching and Assessing: A Revision of Bloom's Taxonomy of Educational Objectives (abridged version)*. New York: Longman.

Assessment Reform Group (2002) *Assessment for Learning: 10 Principles, ARG*. [online] Available at: www.aaia.org.uk/content/uploads/2010/06/Assessment-for-Learning-10-principles.pdf (accessed 30 June 2017).

Black, P, Harrison, C, Hodgen, J, Marshall, B and Serret, N (2010) Validity in Teachers' Summative Assessments. *Assessment in Education: Principles, Policy and Practice*, 17(2): 215–32.

Black, P, Harrison, C, Lee, C, Marshall, B and Wiliam, D (2004) Working Inside the Black Box. *Phi Delta Kappan*, 86(1): 8–21.

Black, P and Wiliam, D (1998) Inside the Black Box: Raising Standards Through Classroom Assessment. *Phi Delta Kappan,* 80(2): 139–48.

Bloom, B S (1956) *Taxonomy of Educational Objectives, Handbook 1: The Cognitive Domain*. New York: David McKay, Co., Inc.

Bramley, T (2007) Paired Comparison Methods, in Newton, P, Baird, J A, Goldstein, H, Patrick, H and Tymms, P (eds) *Techniques for Monitoring the Comparability of Examination Standards*. London: QCA, p 246–300.

Butler, R J and Hardy, L (1992) The Performance Profile: Theory and Application. *The Sport Psychologist,* 6(3): 253–64.

Clarke, S (2005) *Formative Assessment in the Secondary Classroom*. London: Hodder Murray.

Daubney, A (2017) *Teaching Primary Music*. London: SAGE.

Deci, E L and Ryan, R M (1985) *Intrinsic Motivation and Self-determination in Human Behaviour*. New York: Plenum.

Department for Education (DfE) (2013) *The National Curriculum*. London: Crown Publications.

Dunlosky, J, Rawson, K A, Marsh, E J, Nathan, M J and Willingham, D T (2013) Improving Students' Learning with Effective Learning Techniques: Promising Directions from Cognitive and Educational Psychology. *Psychological Science in the Public Interest*, 14(1): 4–58.

Education Endowment Fund (EEF) (2017) *Metacognition and Self-regulation. Teaching and Learning Toolkit*. [online] Available at: https://educationendowmentfoundation.org.uk/resources/teaching-learning-toolkit/ (accessed 29 June 2017).

Eisner, E (1965) Curriculum Ideas in Times of Crisis. *Arts Education*, 18(7): 7–12.

Eisner, E (1996) Overview and Evaluation of Assessment: Conceptions in Search of Practice, in Boughton, D, Eisner, E and Ligtvoet, J (eds) *Evaluating and Assessing the Visual Arts in Education: International Perspectives*. New York: Teachers College Press, pp 1–16.

Fautley, M & Daubney, A (2015) *An Assessment and Progression Framework for Music – Secondary*. London: Incorporated Society of Musicians.

(ISM). [online] Available at: www.ism.org/nationalcurriculumMFAD (accessed 23 August 2017).

Fautley, M and Savage, J (2014) *Lesson Planning for Effective Learning.* Abingdon: Open University Press.

Gardner, J (ed) (2012) *Assessment and Learning* (2nd ed). London: SAGE.

Graue, M (1993) Integrating Theory and Practice Through Instructional Assessment. *Educational Assessment*, 1(4): 283–309.

Harlen, W (2005) Teachers' Summative Practices and Assessment for Learning: Tensions and Synergies. *The Curriculum Journal*, 16(2): 207–23.

Harlen, W and James, M (1997) Assessment and Learning: Differences and Relationships Between Formative and Summative Assessments. *Assessment in Education*, 4(3) 365–79.

Hattie, J (2009) *Visible Learning: A Synthesis of over 800 Meta-analyses Related to Achievement.* New York: Routledge.

Hickman, R (2007) (In Defence of) Whippet-fancying and Other Vices: Re-evaluating Assessment in Art and Design, in Rayment, T (ed) *The Problem of Assessment in Art and Design*. Bristol: Intellect Books UK, NSEAD, p 77–88.

Kelly, G A (1955) *The Psychology of Personal Constructs.* New York: Norton.

Kember, D (no date) *Learning with Digital Portfolios.* [online] Available at: http://education.qld.gov.au/smartclassrooms/documents/strategy/pdf/smart-newsletter.pdf (accessed 29 June 2017).

Koretz, D M (2009) *Measuring Up: What Educational Testing Really Tells Us*. Cambridge, MA: Harvard University Press.

Mansell, W (2007) *Education by Numbers: The Tyranny of Testing.* London: Politico's Publishing.

Ofqual (2015) *A Comparison of Expected Difficulty, Actual Difficulty and Assessment of Problem Solving across GCSE Maths Sample Assessment Materials.* Coventry: Ofqual.

Ofsted (2012) *The Framework for School Inspection from January 2012.* London: Ofsted.

Pirsig, R (1974) *Zen and the Art of Motorcycle Maintenance.* London: Vintage.

Pollard, A, Black-Hawkins, K and Cliff Hodges, G (2014) *Reflective Teaching in Schools.* London: Bloomsbury.

Pollitt, A (2012) The Method of Adaptive Comparative Judgement. *Assessment in Education: Principles, Policy & Practice*, 19(3): 281–300.

Popham, W (2011) *Classroom Assessment: What Teachers Need to Know* (6th ed). Boston, MA: Pearson.

Race, P (2001) *The Lecturer's Toolkit.* London: Kogan Page.

Sadler, D R (1989) Formative Assessment and the Design of Instructional Systems. *Instructional Science*, 18: 119–44.

Sadler, D R (2010) Transforming Holistic Assessment and Grading into a Vehicle for Complex Learning, in Joughin, G (ed) *Assessment, Learning and Judgement in Higher Education*. New York: Springer.

Slavin, R (1983) *Cooperative Learning: Theory, Research and Practice*. Englewood Cliffs, NJ: Prentice-Hall.

Smith, C, Dakers, J, Dow, W, Head, G, Sutherland, M and Irwin, R (2005) A Systematic Review of What Pupils, Aged 11–16, Believe Impacts on Their Motivation to Learn in the Classroom, in *Research Evidence in Education Library*. London: EPPI-Centre, Social Science Research Unit, Institute of Education, University of London.

Spendlove, D (2009) *Ideas in Action: Putting Assessment for Learning into Practice*. London: Continuum.

Stanley, G, MacCann, R, Gardner, J, Reynolds, L and Wild, I (2009) Review of Teacher Assessment: Evidence of What Works Best and Issues for Development. *Oxford University Centre for Educational Assessment Publications*. Oxford: Qualifications and Curriculum Authority.

Stobart, G (2008) *Testing Times: The Uses and Abuses of Assessment*. Abingdon: Routledge.

Stobart, G (2009) Determining Validity in National Curriculum Assessments. *Educational Research*, 51(2): 161–79.

Stoeber, J and Otto, K (2006) Positive Conceptions of Perfectionism: Approaches, Evidence, Challenges. *Personality and Social Psychology Review*, 10: 295–319.

Swann M, Peacock A, Hart, S and Drummond, M J (2012) *Creating Learning Without Limits*. Maidenhead: Open University Press.

Swanwick, K (1999) *Teaching Music Musically*. London: Routledge.

Teacher Assessment in Primary Science (TAPS) (2015). *Introducing the TAPS Pyramid Model*. [online] Available at: https://pstt.org.uk/application/files/6314/5761/9877/taps-pyramid-final.pdf (accessed 26 July 2017).

Townsend, S (1983) *The Secret Diary of Adrian Mole, Aged 13³/₄*. London: Puffin Books.

Vygotsky, L (1978) *Mind in Society*. Cambridge, MA: Harvard University Press.

Wanlin, C M, Hrycaiko, D W, Martin, G L and Mahon, M (1997) The Effects of a Goal-setting Package on the Performance of Speed Skaters. *Journal of Applied Sport Psychology*, 9: 212–28.

Wiliam, D and Black, P (1996) Meanings and Consequences: A Basis for Distinguishing Formative and Summative Functions of Assessment? *British Educational Research Journal*, 22(5): 537–48.

Wood, D, Bruner, J and Ross, G (1976) The Role of Tutoring in Problem Solving. *Journal of Child Psychology and Psychiatry*, 17: 89–100.

CRITICAL
PUBLISHING

Register with Critical Publishing to:

- be the first to know about forthcoming titles;
- find out more about our new Getting it Right in a Week series;
- sign up for our regular newsletter for special offers, discount codes and more.

Visit our website at:

www.criticalpublishing.com